TRUE CRIMES
AND HOW THEY
WERE SOLVED

TRUE CRIMES
AND HOW THEY
WERE SOLVED

Anita Larsen

SCHOLASTIC INC.
New York Toronto London Auckland Sydney

No part of this publication may be reproduced in whole or in part, or stored in a retrieval system, or transmitted in any form or by any means, electronic, mechanical, photocopying, recording, or otherwise, without written permission of the publisher. For information regarding permission, write to Scholastic Inc., 730 Broadway, New York, NY 10003.

ISBN 0-590-46856-1

12 11 10 9 8 7 6 5 4   6 7 8/9

Printed in the U.S.A.   01

First Scholastic printing, December 1993

Contents

Contents

TRUE CRIMES
AND HOW THEY
WERE SOLVED

Introduction:
How Science Began
to Solve Crimes

In the sixteenth century, there were no detectives like the ones we know of today. Criminal investigation meant little more than looking for suspects, with almost no attempt made to find clues. Sometimes officials simply walked away from puzzling crimes — they didn't even try to solve them.

Other times, officials found a scapegoat, a person who might be innocent but who could be accused and punished anyway. The point was to discover *a* culprit rather than *the* culprit. At least this satisfied society that the crime had not gone unpunished.

Standard sixteenth-century procedure was torturing people until they confessed their guilt. Of course, torture was highly effective in producing a speedy confession. This had gone on for hundreds of years, and was thought to be the best way to solve a crime. In fact, before the seventeenth century, great numbers of people believed it was wrong to even *try* solving crimes by using thought and reasoning. That had to change before forensic science, the science of crime solution, could begin to develop.

Once people began to accept the notion that logic was valuable in crime-solving, the field of forensic science began to grow — but slowly. It finally came into its own in the 1800s. That was when authorities began to listen carefully to the information being shouted by the clues left at a crime scene.

The next step forward was taken when detectives realized that much more could be learned from clues if they used new systems to help in analyzing them. One of the earliest systems was Alphonse Bertillion's "anthropometry."

What Bertillion did was simple enough. He took eleven measurements of arrested criminals. The most important of these measurements were the length and width of the criminal's head, middle fingers, and the little finger of the left hand. The odds against misidentification were relatively small since the odds of two people having identical measurements in these four areas are 276 to 1. The odds against misidentification rose to almost 4,000,000 to 1 when seven other measurements were applied. Then Bertillion filed all this data on cards. Each card carried two photos of the person and details of previous arrest records.

Bertillion's system helped solve many crimes by identifying the living, and it provided another benefit, too — identifying the dead. On one occasion a police colleague of Bertillion's, an inspector, asked him to identify a corpse that had been shot several months earlier. The inspector was trying to have some fun by embarrassing the new identification method, but Bertillion believed in his system so firmly that he accepted the challenge.

He gathered measurements, compared them to his file cards, and within minutes handed the inspector the man's name. He added other information he'd taken from his cards. Twelve months earlier the man had been arrested for violent assault. Now that the inspector knew the man's identity, he was able to track down the dead man's friends. And that led him to the arrest of the person who had killed the man after a quarrel about a debt, and thrown his body into the river.

Bertillion's system might be competent, but it was cumbersome — difficult to use. Fortunately, another means of identification was soon discovered — fingerprints. Fingerprints were easier to obtain than all the measurements required by Bertillion's method. They were also easier to keep track of and use.

But even so, the new fingerprint system faced an uphill battle to convince the skeptics. In fact, few advances in forensic science have won acceptance easily. The true cases that follow show how some of the many branches of the forensic sciences developed and grew. They are evidence of the dedication and triumph of forensic scientists, who work in crime labs to help detectives solve seemingly unsolvable crimes.

1
Fingerprinting:
Fingered by Computer

In 1978, San Francisco Police Department Inspector Ken Moses was called to investigate a crime scene. The crime had started out to be a burglary, but it had ended in murder.

The victim was the owner of the home the criminal was attempting to burglarize. The thief didn't stop at taking the woman's possessions. He fired a shot that took her life.

The woman was a survivor of a World War II concentration camp. She had survived the horrors of that death camp only to be shot to death in the "safety" of her own home. The cruel twist of fate made a deep impression on Inspector Moses. He was determined to discover the identity of that intruder.

Inspector Moses was able to lift a fingerprint from the crime scene that he was sure belonged to the suspect. It was almost the only real evidence he could find.

Not willing to give up, Moses carried the fingerprint card from the crime scene with him for the next seven years. In his spare time, he searched the San Francisco Police Department's fingerprint file. His attempt to match one of the thousands of fingerprints on record there with the one on his card was heroic, but he was only one person and the fingerprint file was huge. It could take him the rest of his life to find a matching print and identify the burglar-killer.

Still, finding a match for the crime-scene fingerprint was a reasonable way to proceed. Fingerprints are an undeniable means of identification. One person, and one person only, can leave the fingerprints he or she does.

That's because everybody is born with a unique mark of identity in the pattern of the skin on the tips of the fingers. Here the skin forms papillary ridges you can see under a good light. The patterns of the ridges are classified into arch, loop, and whorl. Dividing these categories into subcategories results in a total of ten categories. Each person's fingerprints make a formula all its own when it is expressed in terms of how it fits into each category.

Another reason fingerprints are so valuable is that, like a leopard's spots, fingerprints can't be changed. In the past, gangsters experimented with ways to "erase" their fingerprints. They used acid and even skin transplants to achieve that. These painful methods had temporary results. The papillary ridges grew back after a time. Even transplanting bits of skin from other parts of the body to the fingers only resulted in other telltale signs.

It is very difficult to avoid leaving fingerprints. Whenever we touch something, we leave them behind.

Why?

Because the papillary ridges of our fingers are lined with sweat pores. Our sweat carries some of the body oils normally found on our fingers, and the oils leave an outline of our ridge pattern when we touch something. Even extremely clean hands leave faint fingerprints, called latent fingerprints. These nearly invisible prints can be "lifted" by various means.

One early way of lifting prints was to brush them with a fine powder, which could then be picked up with transparent tape.

But, since 1982, some crime labs have been lifting prints by other more technical means. One way is by using vapors or fumes of cyanoacrylate, the chemical found in Superglue, for example.

Forensic scientists place the chemical in airtight containers along with the surface containing the fingerprint. As the chemical vapors condense, they stick to the traces of body oils along the fingerprint's ridges, and the print is easily seen. This method is especially useful in developing latent prints found on surfaces most of us wouldn't expect to hold a fingerprint, such as cellophane, aluminum foil — even rubber bands.

An even more high-tech method of finding fingerprints makes use of laser technology. Even if a print is invisible to the naked eye, it can still be seen by a scientist or trained detective wielding a portable laser at a crime scene. The laser light makes the fingerprint visible. Then the print can either be photographed or lifted in some other way.

Scientists can now even take fingerprints from porous surfaces like cloth and skin. Careless disposal of gloves used to avoid leaving fingerprints can result in a fine set of prints that point straight to the criminal!

Although Inspector Moses's search to match the prints on his card with those on record in the San Francisco police file was almost an impossible task, the outcome of the case was astonishing.

Its solution came in early 1985, when Moses's solitary print-comparison attempts received a computer-age boost.

An Automated Fingerprint Identification System (AFIS) was installed on the computers of the San Francisco Police Department. Moses immediately put what had been called his "pet fingerprint" into the system. Only four minutes and ten seconds later his seven-year search was ended! Once the computer had matched Moses's print to another print on file, the suspect's identity was known. With that information, police were able to arrest the man twenty-four hours later.

Thus Inspector Moses added another success story to a long history of murder cases solved through fingerprint evidence. The very first murder case to be solved this way was a case in Argentina in July 1892, solved by a minor police official named

Juan Vucetich. Vucetich was also responsible for the first fingerprint file.

With fingerprinting, as with most advances in criminology, early supporters often faced strong opposition. Vucetich had a tough time convincing his superiors that fingerprinting was the best means of criminal identification. Finally he was able to do so, and Argentina became the first country in the world to base its system of police identification solely on fingerprints.

The value of a fingerprint match in solving a crime has been known for many years. The only drawback until now has been that officials formerly needed a suspect before a fingerprint from a crime scene could be useful in a comparison. The computerized fingerprint file eliminated that need. Instead, it *produced* the suspect!

Since a positive fingerprint identification is accepted as almost ironclad evidence in court, confronting a suspect with that evidence is likely to call forth a confession. That was what happened in Inspector Moses's case. When the suspect was informed of the positive AFIS match, he pleaded guilty to murder. He is now in prison.

Because fingerprint identification was based on comparison, many crime investigators worked to achieve universal fingerprinting — having on record the fingerprints of everybody. Not only could such a practice more easily and readily identify murderers, they said, it would also help in resolving other puzzles of identification.

For example, perhaps an unidentified body — a

"John Doe" or a "Jane Doe" — was a missing person being searched for elsewhere. Two mysteries could be cleared up with a single identification. Victims of accidents or war could also be identified by their fingerprints. So could persons suffering from amnesia, loss of memory. Kidnapped children could also be found and identified this way.

In many ways, fingerprinting everybody and keeping those prints on file made sense. But as useful as universal fingerprinting might sound, many Americans object to it as an invasion of our right to privacy.

There are still those who have concerns about the invasion of a person's privacy through computerized fingerprint systems like AFIS or CAL-ID, the computerized fingerprint system in California. The accuracy of these systems is so great, however, that they reduce the chances of an innocent person being arrested by mistake. And law enforcement agencies using AFIS say the system has also done more to reduce the incidence of crime than any other tool.

The police in Houston, Texas, for example, reportedly solved more than 600 cases in the first year they used AFIS. Police in New Orleans, Louisiana, say they have tripled their success rate in convicting suspects in a crime by being able to match fingerprints accurately. Many other police departments report similar success rates using computerized fingerprint systems.

What's more, law enforcement authorities point out that a higher conviction rate itself lowers the crime rate. Police experts say that the average burglar commits 100 or more burglaries a year. The 1,452 burglars San Francisco police have helped convict since AFIS went into use translates into hundreds of thousands of burglaries that have been prevented.

The system's value in *crime prevention* as well as *crime solving* is shown in a problem case handed to New Orleans police late in 1986. The city was suddenly hit by a wave of violent, random murders. Police felt they were dealing with a serial killer, one of the new breed of killers for whom murder has become an addiction. This one was a man capable of committing a murder every other day. Police knew they needed to find this man quickly in order to save lives.

Authorities got the investigative break they needed the day after Christmas that year — the killer left his fingerprints on a car belonging to two of his victims. Police fed these prints into the computerized system and, within minutes, the system gave them the name of a suspect.

Three days later, that man was arrested. On the evidence of those crime-scene fingerprints, he was undeniably linked to the killings. And those prints also led to his later conviction in four other murders!

Citizens and law enforcement officials would probably all agree that the cost of installing New Orleans' AFIS system had been repaid by just that one case.

And in many other cases, AFIS saves time and money in additional ways. Since there's little defense against fingerprint evidence, defendants often choose not to fight the charges. They prefer to plea bargain, which eases prosecutors' and judges' workloads, frees up badly needed court time, and thus reduces those costs.

Today, fingerprint files — computerized or not — are the bedrock data of many crime laboratories. Many other nations have followed Argentina's 1892 lead in adopting fingerprint identification as the official means of identifying criminals. In 1904, New York City police began, as a matter of course, fingerprinting the people they arrested. The practice spread rapidly to other police departments throughout the United States.

Crime labs, too, began building massive fingerprint files. The first American crime lab opened in Los Angeles in 1923. A second crime lab was established at Northwestern University, in a Chicago suburb, in 1929. On November 24, 1921, the FBI (Federal Bureau of Investigation) opened the first American federal crime lab.

By 1988, twenty states and the District of Columbia had computerized their fingerprint files, and their systems were up and running. Many more states and law enforcement agencies were planning to band together to buy the expensive equipment needed. The FBI's fingerprint bank, the largest in the nation with over 200 million prints, was hoping to modernize its system by 1993 so it could communicate with computers in separate states. Doing so would provide a centralized data bank capable of searching for criminals who have crossed state lines.

Some technology specialists who analyze criminal justice problems say that computerization of fingerprinting is probably the "biggest advancement in law enforcement since the automobile."

Even more intriguing to criminologists is the knowledge that each person's uniqueness, so evident in their fingerprints, is much more than skin deep. Their uniqueness is evident in nearly every shred of their beings. Astonishing as it may sound, a person can often be legally identified through what has come to be called "genetic fingerprinting" — DNA (deoxyribonucleic acid) prints.

2
"Genetic Fingerprinting": The Murder with No Body

The solution to the murder of Helen McCourt is one of the most remarkable cases in all of criminal history — truly a triumph of forensic science. The facts in the case are brief:

On February 9, 1988, twenty-two-year-old Helen McCourt finished work at her job as a computer operator, then took the bus home to Billinge, Merseyside, in England. Her usual pattern was to walk the 300 yards from her bus stop to her home. But that day, her usual pattern was interrupted. McCourt never arrived home.

Police were sure that foul play was involved but were unable to find Helen's body. Without her body, police couldn't prove anything — even that there *had* been a murder.

In the course of their investigation, police came upon the name Ian Simms in Helen's diary. Simms was the owner of the George and Dragon, a local tavern.

Three weeks later, Helen's bloodstained clothes were found in a plastic garbage bag. In a dump three miles away, police found more bloodstained clothing. This time the clothes belonged to Simms. Of course, this pointed to a strong suspicion that Simms had something to do with McCourt's disappearance.

But police were still stymied. Without Helen's body, they couldn't prove that the bloodstains on Simms's clothes were hers. And if they couldn't prove that, they had no case to take to court. And that meant they couldn't take any action against Simms.

Enter forensic science.

Dr. John Moore recalled work done by Dr. Alec Jeffreys of the University of Leicester in 1984. Dr. Jeffreys is not a forensic scientist. He is a geneticist, someone who specializes in the biology of heredity. His work focuses on *d*eoxyribo*n*ucleic *a*cid, a chemical compound called DNA, for short.

DNA is the molecule of heredity; it provides the blueprint that directs the development and maintenance of everyone's bodies. Offspring inherit about half of their DNA from their mother, and about half from their father. DNA appears in the nucleus of every cell in our bodies except red blood cells, which have no nucleus.

Most of these nucleated cells contain 23 pairs of *chromosomes*. These chromosomes are bundles of DNA and contain *genes*. Genes carry coded messages for hereditary characteristics, such as blue eyes or brown eyes. In short, genes determine the unique characteristics of every living thing.

Since we are all human, we have many traits in common. So large strands of DNA are the same in all of us. However, there is a bit of DNA called "junk DNA" that is *not* the same. Unless you're an identical twin, your junk DNA is different from so many other people's junk DNA as to make you unique right down to your molecules. It's the bit of junk DNA that solved the Helen McCourt murder case.

What Dr. Jeffreys contributed to the "chase" for Helen McCourt's murderer is what is sometimes called "a happy accident." While working to develop a process that would reveal the genetic markers for inherited disease, Dr. Jeffreys handed crime investigators an extremely valuable criminal identification technique. He had devised a way to visually identify DNA. And a DNA print of biological clues left at a crime scene can often be as unique as a fingerprint.

Collection and analyses of biological clues at a crime scene is a clean, high-tech process. But it begins in the chaos of violence. Consider an example: A murderer attacks a victim. The victim struggles, wounding the attacker. If enough nucleated white cells of the wounded killer's blood are left on the victim's shirt, investigators can obtain a sample.

DNA prints come from the sample, which is treated with chemicals to break open the white blood cells. DNA is separated from these cells in a complex process that results in a DNA print. The print is a genetic history of an individual person, and it looks rather like a key-punch card.

The DNA print taken from the biological evidence at a crime scene can be compared to one taken from a suspect. That can result in a match as clearcut as the match of two fingerprints. On the other hand, failing to find a match between these two DNA prints can prove that the suspect is innocent.

In the Helen McCourt murder case, Dr. Moore applied this scientific breakthrough to solve the case. Helen was missing, presumed dead. But her parents were still living and could provide blood samples.

Helen's parents were the two people from whom she had obtained the genetic codes that could be matched with DNA prints taken from the bloodstains on Ian Simms's clothing. If investigators could match Helen's parents' DNA prints with a DNA print from the stains on Simms's clothing, it would prove that those bloodstains were Helen's. That would mean they could prove that Simms was very seriously implicated in Helen's death.

The DNA prints did, in fact, establish beyond all doubt that the blood on Simms's clothing was Helen's. Largely on the basis of this evidence, Simms was arrested, tried, convicted, and sentenced to life imprisonment on March 14, 1989.

The use of DNA prints is still relatively new. Many law enforcement officials think it represents a tremendous advance in the tools of criminal investigation. But other criminologists are wary of placing too great a value on DNA prints. They say that such profiles assume too many facts.

One such assumption is that people marry randomly, that they are not bound to their own ethnic group or to one geographical area when they choose a spouse. If the assumption that people marry and have children randomly is true, then only 1 in 1,000,000 people is likely to match the DNA print taken from biological evidence left at a crime scene.

But the detractors of DNA prints say it is *not* true that people marry or reproduce randomly. They say that many people marry within their own ethnic group or subgroup. Among these groups some genetic traits are more common than they are in the population at large — so common that the certainty factor of identification is reduced to perhaps only 1 in 100,000. Some American courts refuse to accept DNA evidence because of this. One in a million is a lot different from one in a hundred thousand!

Another reason some law enforcement officials are wary of the value of DNA prints as evidence in criminal cases is the current lack of testing standards. Strict, nationwide standards for tests that produce DNA prints are needed in order to ensure accurate results.

In early 1992, New York State Governor Mario Cuomo introduced a bill setting up rules for DNA testing in his state. Passage of this, or a similar bill, would make New York the first state in the United States to regulate DNA testing. It would also set up a bank of DNA samples taken from people convicted of murder and sex offenses. Fifteen other states have already created such DNA banks — but not the regulations governing the use of the DNA prints in them.

Since the science is not yet regulated, serious questions arise. Should even a convicted criminal be required to give blood samples? DNA carries many different kinds of information about the blood donor, and making that information available could be an invasion of the tested person's privacy.

Governor Cuomo's proposed bill limits use of the DNA sample to law enforcement purposes. It also provides that the donor can have access to information gained from testing his or her blood sample. It authorizes that the sample must be destroyed if the person's conviction is reversed in the courts.

The benefits and controversies surrounding universal DNA printing are much the same as those that surround universal fingerprinting. The same arguments arise.

DNA printing of all babies shortly after birth would indeed make finding missing children easier — a benefit. But DNA testing of a hair with attached skin cells taken from someone passing out political pamphlets could lead to the identification of that person, who could then be harassed by persons holding opposing political views — a violation of our right to privacy.

This controversy continues, and Dr. Jeffrey's latest DNA-typing technique may add fuel to it. This technique produces a sophisticated digital code that can be stored in a computer, a law enforcement data bank that could be accessed worldwide. Wide-ranging availability of DNA prints escalates the seriousness of the questions already being asked.

Whatever answers surface from this debate and whatever future techniques are discovered, one thing is certain — DNA printing has already earned a respected place in criminal investigations of many kinds.

3
Forensic Pathology: The Case of the Speaking Skeleton

It was 1942. The middle of World War II. For two years, Nazi bombers had steadily blasted away at the London boroughs bordering the River Thames. Lambeth was — and is — one of those boroughs, and Kennington Lane had been especially hard hit. In fact, the Baptist church at 302 Kennington Lane had been totally destroyed.

Demolition workers clearing rubble from the disused graveyard of the ruined church constantly turned up bits of old coffins and skeletons. Each find had to be reported to the South London coroner's office, and no work could be done during the subsequent investigation.

The morning of one hot Friday in July, a workman came across a skull and a few bones that would soon feature heavily in a minor classic in crime detection history. But at the moment, the skeleton was simply a nuisance — one more hitch in the smooth flow of work. The workman sighed and pushed the bones aside, then went to make his report.

Later that afternoon a police van picked up the brown paper bag holding the bones and took it to Southwark morgue where the bones would be routinely autopsied.

The autopsy turned out to be anything but routine.

The next morning, Professor Keith Simpson sifted through the remains. He was England's top Home Office pathologist, working in a forensic science that combines the skills of surgeon and detective. A good pathologist can often solve a case in his lab, and Dr. Simpson was one of the best. His work would not only identify the person whose bones had been found in the graveyard, but it would also identify and help convict the killer responsible for putting the bones there.

The killer hadn't done a very good job of hiding the bones. It may have seemed like a good idea to get rid of the corpse by burying it at the edge of a graveyard, but to do so without putting the body into a coffin first was sure to draw attention and raise questions in the event the body somehow was found.

The absence of a coffin certainly raised questions in Dr. Simpson's mind. Unless the bones were those of a bomb victim, the lack of a coffin indicated that their burial hadn't followed the usual procedures. In addition, the body had been sprinkled with lime. Many people think that lime speeds up the decay of human tissues; forensic professionals know that it actually does the opposite. Lime acts as a preservative.

Dr. Simpson saw at a glance that the bones didn't show the usual signs that appeared on bomb victims. Instead there were signs of another kind; suspicious signs that pointed to purposeful violence. Marks of burning appeared on the skull and rib cage. The lower parts of the arms and legs had been cut off smoothly.

In short, it appeared to Dr. Simpson that the body had been too neatly dismembered to square with the usual effects of an explosion. But to make certain, the doctor had the bones moved to his own laboratory at Guy's Hospital, where he could make a thorough examination.

On Monday morning he carefully cleaned grit and dirt from the skeleton before reassembling the bones. He noted that the body was that of a woman. The size and shape of hipbones and sacrum, the lower five vertebrae of the spine, are different in men and women. So are the skull and leg bones. Dr. Simpson could also tell that the woman had been five feet one inch tall — and she had been dead for about a year or a year and a half.

A patch of scalp containing several strands of dark brown, graying hair still clung to the skull. Examination of the skull vault sutures — fine crevices in the bones of the skull that close completely at about age twenty-five — told Dr. Simpson that the woman was older than that. From evidence like the graying hair and his experience with racial characteristics, Dr. Simpson calculated the woman's age as being between forty-five and sixty years at the time of her death.

Examination of the woman's skull told Dr. Simpson something else, too. Marks appearing at the base of the skull were similar to the marks at her elbows and knees, which meant that the woman's head had also been severed.

The lime the killer had used in an attempt to destroy the body had instead given Dr. Simpson a useful investigative gift. It had preserved the tiny bones of the woman's voice box and patches of skin on her throat. The voice box had been crushed, and the skin on her throat showed signs of bruising. These two conditions pointed to a cause of death. The woman had been strangled.

Lime had also preserved much of the woman's lower abdomen. There, Dr. Simpson found a fibroid tumor. That could be of immense help in identifying her, as could her upper jaw. Four teeth remained in the jaw, all with dental work. Once the investigation had gotten to the stage of producing some possible names for the skeleton, comparisons of medical and dental records would narrow the field. Perhaps they would even provide a direct and conclusive identity.

After Dr. Simpson concluded that the woman had been strangled to death and then dismembered, he called police. Their next step was to compile a list of all women who had been reported missing in the past two years. Then they began to wade through the investigation of those names.

Some weeks later, police came up with a likely

name — Mrs. Rachael Dobkin. She had been reported missing by her sister in April 1941, eighteen months earlier. That fit the outside range of Dr. Simpson's date-of-death estimate. Rachael's dark-brown hair had begun to gray, and she was five feet one inch tall. Just before she disappeared, the woman had complained of abdominal pain. Doctors had diagnosed a fibroid tumor of the womb, which Rachael had refused to have removed.

Hearing this news, Dr. Simpson felt certain that the skeleton was that of Rachael Dobkin. To make sure, he asked police to get the dead woman's dental records. Happily enough, this didn't prove difficult. Rachael's sister knew the name of her dentist, and his records were ordered. When the records came, they were an identical match to the work done on the Lambeth skull.

Although the skeleton's identity had now been proven beyond a doubt, Dr. Simpson went one step further. He got a picture of the dead woman, had it blown up to life size, and superimposed it on the skull. A perfect match.

So the heap of bones now had a name. And examination of the bones had disclosed the final event in the woman's history — she had died a violent death.

An even bigger boon for police was that Dr. Simpson's autopsy had provided much information about the killer. Mrs. Dobkin had been strangled by a person with a powerful grip, probably a man.

There were traces of clotted blood on the back of her skull. These indicated that her killer was strong. Within hours of the murder, judging by the blood clots and the straight scars on the remaining bones, the killer had cut off the woman's head, forearms, and lower parts of the legs. He had tried to burn the torso, but had given up, finally resorting to burying the remains in lime.

What did all this tell Dr. Simpson about the killer? He was strong. He was unimaginative. And he had been desperate, pushed to the limit.

Why might he have killed Rachael Dobkin? What could the killer's motive have been?

The killer had probably been someone she knew well, someone on whom she had a hold of some kind.

For many years, investigators in murder cases tended to suspect spouses. That is changing now, because the nature of killers is changing. But in 1942, Dr. Simpson's profile of Rachael Dobkin's killer led police to investigate her estranged husband, Harry.

According to Rachael's sister, Harry had deserted his wife some years earlier. After that, Rachael lived alone, and there was no indication that she and Harry had ever seen each other again. But Rachael's sister did mention that there had been some trouble over alimony payments. . . .

Police checked the records of the local magistrate's courts. These courts had jurisdiction over questions concerning alimony. Police discovered that some months before, Harry Dobkin had fallen behind on his alimony payments and been jailed. As soon as he came out of prison, Rachael had been there to badger him.

At the same time, other inquiries were turning up the information that Harry Dobkin was a construction worker and that he had had little education.

An official search for Harry had begun concurrently with the rest of the police investigation. It was conducted with orders not to alarm the man. Since there had been no newspaper coverage of the case, police hoped to find Harry quickly and quietly.

That is exactly what happened. Harry Dobkin was living in south London, only a few miles away from Lambeth. About the time Rachael Dobkin had probably died, her husband had been "firewatching" in Kennington Lane. During the war, fire-watchers helped spot fires started by bombs.

Police asked the man to call at the Southwark police station "on a minor matter." He came in. He was a heavily built man with powerful arms and shoulders. Police looked at him and recalled Dr. Simpson's profile — "Strong, unimaginative, and very desperate."

Dobkin was arrested for the murder of his wife on the spot, and a jury later found him guilty. He was hanged in Wandsworth Prison on a morning just before Christmas, 1942.

The "silent witnesses" Dr. Simpson brought to bear in testimony in this case are dramatic. A heap of bones spoke of savagery that had taken place at least a year earlier, perhaps even longer. Their long silence was finally broken by a forensic pathologist working hand in hand with police.

Police can now call on other forensic specialists

to "put flesh" on dead bones. Forensic sculptors can help crime investigators see what a long-dead person looked like when alive. These medical artists can reconstruct a three-dimensional sculpture of a face from a skull by using the known thickness of flesh over different parts of the skull.

And new computer software programs are also proving helpful. Such programs can reconstruct a person's face from the skull. These programs can also "age" a face or show what it looked like when the person was younger. This data is useful in showing how a child who has been missing for several years, or a criminal who has been hiding for years, might look today.

Use of such photos on TV shows such as *America's Most Wanted* and *Unsolved Mysteries* have led to a number of arrests. Neighbors and acquaintances have recognized someone they know and phoned tips to police.

4
Forensic Ballistics:
The St. Valentine's
Day Massacre

Chicago was lawless in the 1920s. If anybody made and enforced the rules in that city, it was the notorious bootleg gangs.

The gangs were run by violent men whose names have become synonymous with organized crime — Johnny Torrio and his young assistant Alphonse "Scarface Al" Capone, Dion O'Bannion and his chief lieutenant Hymie Weiss, Bugs Moran, and others.

Alcohol was the lifeblood of these gangs. The federal government prohibited the sale and use of alcohol in the twenties, but the gangs defied those laws. They kept a stream of bootleg liquor flowing, and gang bosses controlling this stream of alcohol became fabulously wealthy. So much money could be made at bootlegging, in fact, that the gangs were ruthless in protecting the territories they had staked out.

On November 8, 1924, for example, the Torrio-Capone gang eliminated its major rival, Dion O'Bannion, in a typically cold-blooded way. While one gang member shook O'Bannion's hand in peace, others riddled him with bullets.

A gangland murder like this led to vows of vengeance. The vows led to other murders. The new murders brought forth further vows of vengeance, and on and on the cycle went. The gangs could get away with such mayhem because many police and city officials looked the other way.

But on the morning of February 14, 1929, a gangland massacre occurred that couldn't be swept under the rug.

That Valentine's Day morning, seven of Bugs Moran's best men had gathered in a garage on North Clark Street. The Bugs Moran gang controlled bootlegging on Chicago's North Side, and his men were at the garage to wait for a shipment of liquor expected to arrive that morning. The men also expected their boss Bugs to show up for that shipment.

What arrived at the garage instead were two men in Chicago police uniforms. At 10:30 AM the "uniforms" entered the garage with their guns drawn. They ordered Bugs's men to line up against the wall.

Suddenly, two men in civilian clothes appeared behind the two uniformed men. The latecomers pulled submachine guns from beneath their coats and fired a hail of bullets. After mowing down the line of Bugs Moran's men in a businesslike manner, they calmly left the scene, got into a car, and disappeared.

Bugs Moran showed up at the garage late. He escaped the slaughter.

Chicago coroner Dr. Herman N. Bundesen turned up still later, after Bugs had left the scene. In the garage, Bundesen found six corpses, one dying man, and seventy spent submachine-gun cartridges.

Everybody in the know knew that the massacre was the work of Al Capone. It was Scarface Al's way of eliminating his last major business competitor. Capone had been careful to be out of town at the time of the massacre, although witnesses had seen some of his men around the garage. But no real evidence against Capone's men — Jack McGurn, Fred Burke, and Freddie Goetz — could be gathered, so no real action could be taken against either them or their boss.

Coroner Bundesen knew that the honest cops in Chicago wouldn't get a great deal of support in investigating this case, so he looked for other ways to make sure action would be taken. It was within his powers to call a grand jury. A grand jury's job is to look at the evidence in a criminal situation and determine if there are sufficiently strong and legal reasons to insist on further investigation.

Bundesen's grand jury was composed of wealthy citizens independent of the political structure, which included the police department. His jury looked at the evidence collected from the garage on North Clark Street and decided to call in an expert on forensic ballistics.

Ballistics is, strictly speaking, the mathematical

study of the flight of objects thrust into space. But the popular meaning of the word has come to mean the investigation of bullets from guns used in shooting cases.

The premier forensic ballistics expert in the 1920s was Calvin Goddard, who worked in New York City. The St. Valentine's Day Massacre was the kind of case Goddard liked. It had gotten media coverage all over the nation, and so would the person who solved it. Goddard hoped that working on the case — and solving it — would be a giant step toward fulfilling one of his longtime dreams. He wanted to see the creation of a national laboratory for scientific criminology.

In particular, Goddard wanted a laboratory so respected that its work could establish serious regard for the relatively new science of forensic ballistics, a laboratory that could develop controls and do solid research. He had seen much incompetence and foolishness in the courtroom testimony of so-called ballistic experts in the past, cases in which innocent people had been convicted because of "expert" information that was incorrect, pure and simple.

Though the science of forensic ballistics was relatively new, it had been used in crime-solving as far back as the eighteenth century. At the time, most guns were the kind that had to be "broken" so each individual charge could be loaded. This was done by putting gunpowder and a ball of lead into the gun's muzzle. The charge was then packed down with paper wadding. The powder was ignited by a spark made when the gun's hammer struck some flint at the back end of a barrel that was, at first, smoothly bored.

It was the wadding that led to the first solution of a crime achieved through ballistics. The case centered on a shooting that took place in England in 1784.

The victim was a man named Edward Culshaw. He had been shot by someone using a flintlock pistol. The paper wadding used to pack down the charge had been torn from a street ballad, a popular song printed like a sheet of newspaper and distributed by hand. A teenager named John Toms was the prime suspect in the case. When officials searched Toms, they found the rest of the sheet of music in his pocket. The tear in that sheet matched the piece torn off to be used as wadding in the murder weapon. That was enough evidence to convict Toms of the crime.

The Toms case was an unusual one, however, and although evidence from guns continued to be used in criminal investigations from time to time, it wasn't until 1820 that *modern* forensic ballistics became possible or even especially useful.

The reason? The invention of the percussion cap, a metal cap that exploded when struck with the hammer of a firearm. The percussion cap eliminated the need to use loose powder to fire a shot. These charges made firearms much easier to handle, and use of them spread rapidly.

An even more important step in the spread of firearms was taken by a young man from Hartford,

Connecticut, named Samuel Colt. Colt invented the revolver, a handgun that took its name from a revolving chamber holding bullets. The chamber rotated when the handgun's hammer was cocked. The advantage of this to a shooter was, of course, speed. He could get off six shots without reloading instead of having to reload with every shot. The Texas Rangers needed a weapon like this, and Colt was happy to meet the demand. By 1846 he and a business partner were mass-producing the revolvers.

The Colt revolver was not a hunting gun. It was a weapon made to shoot people and it was advertised as such. The ads called the Colt revolver "the equalizer," and that name provided powerful motivation for many who lived on America's western frontier to buy the six-shooter. Even more motivation to buy one of the handguns was the six-shooter's reliability. Add all that to the inexpensiveness of the gun, and Colt's factory was soon turning out and selling thousands of the revolvers a day. It was the first mass-produced article offered to the American people, and its use spread quickly to other nations, as well.

Meanwhile, other gunmakers had come up with further refinements in firearms. They found that the accuracy of a bullet could be improved if the barrel contained spiraled grooves. Lead balls shot from old muskets became more wildly inaccurate the farther away the target was, but rifling the barrel — making five to seven spiral grooves in the gun barrel — made a bullet shot from it spin about its axis. This spinning helped the bullet fly straight and true.

A rifled barrel did something else that was of particular interest to investigators. Rifling a gun barrel caused it to mark each bullet fired from it, leaving its "fingerprint" in the process.

The markings, called "striations," are made as the bullet travels down the barrel. The shell that remains in the gun will retain scratches made by the firing pin. Both firing pin and barrel marks are unique for each gun.

In the late 1800s, a brilliant French criminalist, Alexandre Lacassagne, recognized that these unique "fingerprints" could be useful in crime investigations. Unfortunately he was largely ignored.

The rightful place of ballistics in criminal investigation was mentioned again in a lecture given at a Congress of Legal Medicine held in Paris in May 1912. This time the information would fall, sooner or later, into the fertile mind of American Charles E. Waite, an employee of the New York State Prosecutor.

Waite had become interested in the science of firearm indentification as a result of a case of criminal prosecution gone wrong. An innocent man had been convicted of a murder because of inept "expert" ballistics evidence. Waite decided to keep such miscarriages of justice from ever happening again, and set himself an ambitious task. He would study and identify the markings left by every known firearm.

He worked for years and was making good progress until he suddenly realized that his work was a fool's project. True, each gun left a unique pattern of marks useful in identifying the firearm from which a bullet had been fired, but cataloging every gun that had been, or would ever be, produced was impossible. Even if it had been possible, anything useful to criminal investigators would be buried in the huge heap of once and future data.

So Waite decided to take hold of the other end of the stick. If he couldn't catalog every last firearm, some of which hadn't even been made yet, he *could* find a way to study every important bullet that was fired. An important bullet, of course, was one that had been used in a crime.

With physicist John H. Fischer and chemist Philip O. Gravelle, Waite set up the Bureau of Forensic Ballistics in New York. A couple of important and highly useful inventions came from this collaboration. One was the helixometer, invented by Fischer. This was a hollow probe fitted with a lamp and a magnifying glass. It solved the problem of looking down gun barrels.

The other invention — the comparison microscope — was Gravelle's. By using this instrument, the halves of two separate bullet images could be joined together under the same lens. This allowed a comparison of the marks on each, a comparison that quickly showed if a particular gun had shot the bullets found at a crime scene, or not.

With the inventions of the helixometer and comparison microscope in 1923, the science of ballistics was born in the laboratory.

In 1925, Waite acquired his third collaborator, an army ex-colonel and medical officer named Calvin Goddard. When Waite died later the next year, Goddard stepped into his shoes to become the world's foremost ballistics expert. And this, four years later, resulted in the call from the Chicago grand jury that was looking into the St. Valentine's Day Massacre.

Soon after Goddard answered that call, he would become the first director of a national crime lab in America. Two wealthy members of the grand jury offered to finance a crime lab at Northwestern University, which was located in a Chicago suburb. The members of the grand jury asked Goddard to direct the lab and he was happy to agree. During his work there, Goddard wrote *History of Firearms Identification*, which was published in 1936 and is still the classic work on the subject. But that work was still in the future.

The first thing Goddard did when he arrived in Chicago was examine all the evidence collected in the St. Valentine's Day Massacre. That evidence included all the shells and bullets found in the victims' bodies as well as those taken from the garage on North Clark Street.

The grand jury waited anxiously for Goddard's opinion, and they soon had it.

The job, Goddard said, had been done with two .45-caliber Thompson submachine guns. One of these was the magazine type with twenty bullets to a loading. The other was the drum type with a loading of fifty shots.

Police were also given this information, but it didn't take them much further along toward solving the crime until they had a stroke of luck.

On December 14, 1929, a policeman in St. Joseph, Michigan, stopped a car for a traffic offense. The bad driver shot the policeman and sped away.

But the policeman had taken the car's license number, and the traffic offender's address was traced through that. A search of his apartment gave police a real shock. In addition to bad driving habits, the man who lived in the apartment had an arsenal of weapons . . . including two Thompson submachine guns!

The "tommy guns" were sent to Goddard immediately. Test bullets were fired into containers of cotton, and Goddard studied them under his microscope. That examination led him to conclude that these guns were the very ones used in the St. Valentine's Day Massacre.

A few days later, the bad driver in Michigan was caught. He turned out to be none other than Fred Burke, one of the Capone gangsters who had been under suspicion from the start. Burke had been hiding out and using an alias, or false name.

Burke was convicted and sentenced to life imprisonment. That left the other two police suspects in the case, Freddie Goetz and Jack McGurn, free to go where they wished. But the two didn't go far. Bugs Moran and his gang took care of them in their own way. The two gangsters were found mysteriously shot to death.

The threat of gangland reprisal followed Goddard, as well. For years he worked with a revolver at his belt in the laboratory he had established at Northwestern University. An armed guard was always stationed in the hall. Each time a shot was fired, even if it were only one of Goddard's test shots, the guard looked into the room.

When Goddard finally left the Northwestern laboratory at the end of 1934, another of his dreams was on the verge of being realized. J. Edgar Hoover was setting up a special department of forensic ballistics in the crime lab he directed, the Federal Bureau of Investigation. The science of ballistics had spread to other places, too. Most major European crime labs instituted separate ballistics departments in the 1930s.

Compared with criminal identification systems like fingerprinting or DNA printing, the identification of weapons used criminally has limitations. A bullet distorted by impact is almost impossible to match, for example. And although every gun has its own "fingerprint," there is no way for investigators to track down what specific firearm shot a specific bullet if they don't already have it. By and large, ballistics experts need to have the weapon that fired the bullet in order for their scientific experience to be useful in gathering evidence.

When a shotgun has been used in a crime, the ballistic expert's identification problems are expanded. Although an identification can be made in some cases, a shotgun fires a sprinkling of shot from a shell rather than a single bullet or slug from the barrel of the weapon.

Still, the science of forensic ballistics has proven its worth. Ballistic evidence has convicted criminals of the crimes they've committed and proved the innocence of persons wrongfully accused.

5
Forensic Toxicology:
The Elizabeth Barlow Case

Poison.

It was the preferred means of murder in the seventeenth century. Crime investigators throughout that century and much of the next bemoaned the difficulties they faced in compiling solid scientific data about poisons, the kind of data that would stand up in court as evidence.

Then in 1840 a murder took place that started to change all that. Marie Lafarge's loutish husband died in a small town in a French province. Marie was accused of using arsenic she'd bought "for the rats," as it was put in later testimony in court. One of the outcomes of this case was that the testimony of toxicologists — those who are expert in the science of poisons — was thrust into prominence. Forensic toxicology was given new stature and respect as a science.

By the 1950s, toxicology had become a vast and intricate structure. The foundations of the science had been built steadily and sturdily over the past centuries, and those firm foundations were necessary. The science of poisons has to keep running in order to stay in the same place. As soon as one poisonous substance yields its secrets to toxicologists, it is replaced by thousands of others that flow from the laboratories of chemists and pharmacologists.

The growth of drugs and chemicals was necessary and useful in the Industrial Age. But there was a flip side to the invention of all these useful drugs and chemicals. Many of them were potentially deadly . . . and almost everyone could now easily put their hands on a wealth of new poisons.

But if forensic toxicologists have had to scurry to keep up with the rapidly multiplying kinds and numbers of poisons since the beginning of the twentieth century, they do have one thing working for them — collaboration. Combating what could become a flood of poisonings called for close collaboration between the laboratory and the police, and that collaboration is what finally solved the murder of Elizabeth Barlow.

Elizabeth Barlow died on the night of May 3, 1957. By that time, toxicologists and toxicological laboratories had become an integral part of most nations' detective forces.

Shortly before midnight on that May night, a doctor phoned Detective Sergeant Naylor of the Criminal Investigation Division of Bradford City in England. While making a house call to a residence on Thornbury Crescent, the doctor had found something suspicious.

The doctor said that at about 11:30 PM, a couple named Skinner had called him. The Skinners expressed concern about one of their neighbors, Elizabeth Barlow.

The doctor had come to the Thornbury Crescent row house to find Mrs. Barlow dead in the bathtub. He immediately phoned police, reaching Naylor, who said he'd come right away.

Naylor arrived at the row house, which was typical of such homes. There was a living room and kitchen on the ground floor, and a bedroom and bath upstairs. Naylor found the doctor waiting at the head of the stairs with the dead woman's husband, Kenneth, a man about thirty-eight.

Kenneth Barlow was a male nurse. He worked at St. Luke's, a hospital in a nearby town. Barlow looked on silently as the doctor led Naylor to the bathroom.

Elizabeth Barlow, a small woman about thirty, lay in the now drained tub. Her arms were bent as if she were asleep. There was no indication of violence.

But Naylor noticed something that could point to foul play. The woman's pupils were widely dilated. The doctor, too, had noticed this; it was what had made him suspicious enough to call the police. He had instantly assumed that Mrs. Barlow had been under the influence of a drug of some kind at the time of her death. Now, the doctor told Naylor that the presence of some drug in the woman's body had only been his assumption.

When the doctor left on another call, Kenneth Barlow told Naylor his story. He spoke smoothly and without hesitation. This had been his day off from the hospital, he said, and also his wife's day off from her work in a laundry.

During the afternoon, she had begun to feel ill. She went to bed, asking her husband to call her at 7:30 PM, in time for a television program she wanted to see. When he'd done so, Barlow said, his wife said she'd decided she didn't want to see the program after all. She was feeling comfortable where she was.

Two hours later, Elizabeth called out to say she had been sick. Her husband changed the bedclothes, then went to bed himself.

Soon Elizabeth complained of feeling too warm and said she was going to take a bath to cool off and relax. Kenneth dozed off, waking again shortly after 11:00 PM. He was alone in their bedroom. His wife had not come back to bed.

The light was still on in the bathroom. He went there to see if his wife was all right. She wasn't. She seemed to have drowned in the bathtub. Barlow tried to pull her from the water, but couldn't. She was limp, too heavy. He drained the water from the tub and tried to revive her with artificial respiration. His efforts failed.

Naylor listened to this story, then looked around the apartment for anything that would be useful to forensic scientists if they were called in on the case.

The pajamas Barlow had worn while trying to save his wife were in the bedroom. They were completely dry.

Those dry pajamas were the only jarring note. Everything else Naylor saw supported Barlow's story.

But that one jarring note was insistent and troublesome. How could those pajamas be dry if it was true that Barlow tried to lift his wife from the water as he claimed?

Naylor decided to phone Chief Constable H. S. Price. When he reached Price, Naylor said he thought the Harrogate police laboratory should be informed. That sounded serious enough that Price decided he'd better take a look. It didn't take him long to arrive. Price was at the Barlows' row house ten minutes after he hung up the phone.

Once there, Price found further inconsistencies in Barlow's story. One thing in particular struck him as odd. Barlow claimed he had attempted to pull his wife from a full bathtub, but there were no splashes of water on the walls or the floor of the bathroom.

This and other peculiar things led Chief Constable Price to agree wholeheartedly with his sergeant — Harrogate should be called.

It didn't take long for Harrogate forensic specialists to arrive. Two Harrogate men were at the Barlow row house by 3:30 AM. One of the men was Chief Inspector Coffey, who had been on night duty at the lab when the call came. The other was the pathologist and forensic scientist Dr. David Price.

Two pairs of keen eyes, experienced in assessing a crime scene, noted further inconsistencies in Barlow's story.

It was Chief Inspector Coffey who found suspicious evidence in the kitchen. He spotted two hypodermic needles. One of the syringes was wet. Did that wet syringe contain some traces of a lethal drug Barlow might have injected into his wife?

Barlow immediately offered an explanation for the syringes. He was a nurse, he reminded the authorities. Naturally he would have syringes around the house. He had a good explanation of why one of the syringes was wet, too. He had indeed used it for an injection. But he hadn't given his wife a shot. Instead, he had injected some penicillin into himself to help him get rid of a carbuncle, or boil, that had been bothering him.

In short, Barlow flatly denied having given his wife an injection of any kind. But Dr. Price looked again at the dead woman's eyes.

Her dilated pupils strongly indicated Elizabeth had been under the influence of some sort of drug. On the basis of evidence at the crime scene, the scientist and police officers all agreed in feeling that something was terribly wrong with Barlow's story. They ordered the woman's body to be taken to Harrogate that same night.

The remains of Elizabeth Barlow arrived at the Harrogate crime lab at 5:40 AM. Dr. Price at once started his investigation into the woman's death. He performed an autopsy, a physical examination of a dead person. He was looking for physical signs that could point to the cause of the sudden onset of weakness Barlow had said his wife experienced before she died.

But Dr. Price found nothing unusual. Elizabeth's heart was sound; so were all her other organs. Her pancreas, thyroid, and pituitary glands were normal. There were no signs of infection in her body, and no injection marks on her skin. Elizabeth had been about two months pregnant, but her pregnancy was normal. By the time he'd finished the autopsy, Price had come no closer to knowing why Elizabeth Barlow died. He had found no medical reason for the woman to have fainted in the bathtub and drowned.

There was another plausible explanation of what had happened, and Dr. Price turned that explanation over in his mind. Had Elizabeth Barlow been poisoned? It seemed to be the only possible answer to this mystery.

But Price needed expert advice to arrive at that answer. He called A. S. Curry of the Home Office Forensic Science Laboratory, and P. H. Wright of the Department of Chemical Pathology at Guy's Hospital Medical School.

Curry and Wright began lengthy scientific analyses. They wanted to know if they could detect medicines and poisons in the dead woman's body. They tested her digestive tract, analyzed samples of her organs and body fluids. They performed all the well-known tests for several hundred different medicines and poisons. None of these tests produced results that pointed to the presence of any known

47

poisons or medicines in Elizabeth Barlow's body.

Having eliminated those possibilities, the scientists took another tack. They employed all the biochemical tests and methodologies that could show if Elizabeth Barlow had a blood disease or a metabolic disturbance.

Again, the scientists came up with nothing. They found no trace of a blood disease or any disruption of the way Elizabeth Barlow's body was working. Nothing at all that might have caused Elizabeth's sudden weakness and subsequent drowning came to light.

Next, the scientists turned to an examination of the hypodermic syringes and needles taken from the Barlow house. To mystify the case even further, they found only tiny traces of penicillin on one of them. That evidence confirmed Barlow's story that he had injected penicillin into himself.

Was the whole investigation at a dead end?

A frustrated but determined Dr. Price couldn't accept that.

Four days later, Dr. Price still couldn't shake off the strong sense that Elizabeth Barlow had died while under the influence of some kind of drug. He refused to stop his efforts until he had learned what that drug might have been.

The first step for Price was to determine definitely if Elizabeth Barlow had been injected. To do that, he searched over the entire surface of the woman's body for the injection marks a hypodermic needle would leave. Just as Sherlock Holmes might have done, Dr. Price used a magnifying glass and the illumination of a strong light.

After two hours of concentrated searching, Dr. Price met with success. He found what he was looking for — two tiny marks close together on Elizabeth Barlow's left side and two similar dotlike marks on her right side. The woman's freckles and moles had masked these marks effectively until now.

Were these injection tracks?

To learn that, Dr. Price carefully cut through the tissues at the side of the marks. He found the tiny inflammations or marks of swelling that are usually left by fresh injections. The injection mark on Elizabeth Barlow's left side had been made only hours before her death.

Those marks were the first positive evidence that Kenneth Barlow's story could be a lie. From the placement of the injection marks, he *had* injected something into his wife — and whatever it was might have caused her death!

But, Price asked himself, what had the man used?

There was no point in asking Barlow. The man would claim that he had injected his wife with vitamins! And with the evidence Dr. Price had gathered to this point in his investigation, there was no way that such a claim could be disproved.

But there were other avenues of investigation that might show what substance Barlow had used. He could be watched, for one thing. And his nursing work at St. Luke's Hospital could be looked into.

What medicines had Barlow had at his disposal? Had any disappeared?

Dr. Price stored in his lab refrigerator the pieces of Elizabeth Barlow's tissues that bore the injection marks. Perhaps minute traces of whatever had been injected into the woman could be extracted from the injection sites. The amount of tissue was so small that extreme care had to be taken. The bits of tissue could be used only when scientists were pretty sure of what they were looking for. Further tests and procedures had to be undertaken carefully. Results of those tests should be used for confirmation rather than discovery.

Curry and Price knew that they needed more help on this case. They decided to call experts into the forensic collaboration. Professor C. S. Russell, gynecologist of Sheffield University; Professor R. H. Thompson, head of the Department of Chemical Pathology at Guy's Hospital in London and S. S. Randall of the Biochemical Department of the Boots Pure Drug Co. Ltd., of Nottingham joined the search for the truth about Elizabeth Barlow's death.

The question Curry and Price put to the experts they'd called in was this: What drug or medicine could have produced in a woman in the first stages of pregnancy the symptoms that were reported in Elizabeth Barlow — fatigue, vomiting, sweating, sudden weakness, unconsciousness, wide dilation of the pupils of the eyes?

What these symptoms suggested to all the experts was hypoglycemia. This condition occurs when the sugar content of the blood is lowered. Blood sugar must remain at a certain level to sustain life. A healthy person's body regulates its own blood sugar. When sugar is taken in a form like candy, the body shuts down its own natural sugar production.

Elizabeth Barlow was healthy. If a healthy person were given too much sugar, say in the form of an injection of a hormone called insulin, then the result would soon be a lack of enough sugar-energy to run the body. Unless the person were given an immediate dose of glucose, or sugar in a form that dissolves in a liquid like blood, death would follow.

The notion that Barlow, a trained nurse, might have hit on a new murder method — injecting insulin into his healthy wife — occurred to the experts. But it was only a vague notion, and they pushed it aside.

But the vague notion was insistent. It kept coming back.

Perhaps the reason that the nagging notion kept returning to the scientists was a second piece of curious evidence that had surfaced during routine biochemical tests conducted on the body. Curry had removed mixed blood from the two chambers of Elizabeth Barlow's heart. When he examined this blood for its sugar content, he found 210 milligrams of blood sugar to each 100 milliliters of blood. This amount of blood sugar was much higher than normal.

If Barlow *had* discovered a new way to kill, had he also timed his murder so that the inevitable coma would come when Elizabeth was in the bath? Had he known she would drown if that happened? Had he lain in his bedroom, waiting and counting the minutes until his unconscious wife would slip down in the tub, until she would begin to breathe not air, but deadly water . . . ?

On a scientific level, the nagging questions gained force on May 23 when Chief Constable Price, who had been on the case almost from the beginning, came to Harrogate. He had gathered information through traditional police investigative techniques, like asking questions.

The chief constable reported that there was indeed something fishy about Barlow. The man's first wife — Elizabeth was his second — had died in 1956, the year before Elizabeth's death. There had been an air of mystery about the death of Barlow's first wife, too. No plausible cause for it had ever been discovered.

In addition, a nurse at St. Luke's had been questioned. She said that Barlow was often in charge of giving insulin injections at the hospital.

The forensic scientists' ears perked up. Barlow had had the opportunity to murder his second wife. He and Elizabeth had been alone at home on the night of her death. Now they were hearing that the man had had the means to do so. He could easily have gotten the necessary insulin and then used his specialized knowledge to prepare and administer a lethal dose of a hormone that had given the promise of life to so many other people, those afflicted with the disease of diabetes.

Two legs of the triad that crime investigators look for — opportunity and method — had suddenly appeared. The remaining leg was motive; the reason why a crime was committed. And Kenneth Barlow's motive in murdering his wife could be determined once the commission of a crime was proven.

As Chief Constable Price continued his report, more seemingly strong evidence against Barlow piled up. Barlow had once worked at the Northfield Sanatorium. In the course of a conversation with a patient there, Barlow had said that a "real dose" of insulin would result in death.

If he had injected his wife with insulin, Kenneth Barlow had known exactly what would happen.

Another of Barlow's reported conversations had suspicious overtones, too. Around Christmas, 1955, while talking with a fellow male nurse, Barlow said that insulin could be used to commit the perfect crime. He said that insulin would never be detected because it dissolved in the blood and left no trace.

If he had injected his wife with insulin, Kenneth Barlow had planned her death. If it had been a premeditated murder — then he had also planned to escape punishment for his crime.

Chief Constable Price's information was so strong that on the same day it was delivered, Elizabeth Barlow's tissues came out of Dr. Price's laboratory refrigerator. If Barlow had injected his wife with insulin, traces of that hormone would be found at the injection sites, or not at all. What needed to be done to help insure that Barlow would be brought to justice was to identify the hormone in those injection-site tissues.

But that was not going to be easy.

A search of the scientific literature of forensic medicine, toxicology, and biochemistry had led to a blank wall. It appeared that no one had ever before murdered another person with insulin, a relatively new invention at the time. For the forensic scientists, there was no path to follow in the detection of insulin in Elizabeth Barlow's tissues.

In fact, the only bit of scientific knowledge the scientists working on the Elizabeth Barlow case found seemed to give substance to her husband's innocence. A paper published in 1940 reported results on experiments to determine blood-sugar values in corpses. The finding explained why Curry had found so much sugar — 210 milligrams — in Elizabeth Barlow's heart.

The 1940 research showed that the amount of sugar in mixed heart blood had no bearing on the amount of sugar in the blood as a whole. In thirty-eight healthy people who had died violently from suffocation or drowning, the earlier researchers had found unusually high sugar values in the right chamber of the heart, while the rest of the dead person's blood had extremely low levels of sugar.

The explanation?

At the moment of death, the liver, which is the body's sugar storehouse, had mobilized its last reserves and flung them into the bloodstream in a last attempt to preserve life. These reserves, the early researchers found, had just enough time to travel through the blood stream as far as the right chamber of the heart before the person died. The sugar stayed in the heart because the heart stopped beating at death and no longer circulated blood.

The scientists working on the Barlow case were dismayed by this news but not deterred. A method of identifying insulin in human tissues had not yet been devised, but that didn't mean it was impossible. After all, the chemical structure of insulin had been known since 1955; it was just the chemical tests to identify it in body tissues that were missing from the toxicological record.

Curry decided to do comparison tests of biological activity to find those chemical tests. This was a time-consuming approach, but a time-honored one.

First, a control group of mice were injected with various amounts of insulin. Doses of insulin are measured in internationally standardized units in their use as a control of diabetes. Careful observation of the mice's reactions were noted as the symptoms familiar to the investigators in the Barlow case appeared — trembling, twitching, restlessness, weakness, coma, finally death.

The information from this control group of mice could now be compared to information gained in the next stage, in which extracts from the injection sites on Elizabeth Barlow's tissues were prepared. Doses of these extracts were injected into other mice. These mice displayed exactly the same symptoms as the control mice had. They fell into a coma and died.

This was the proof the scientists had been looking

for. Elizabeth Barlow had indeed been injected with insulin.

But there was even more information to be learned from this first comparison test. Some of the extracts were stronger than others. When Dr. Price had first found the injection marks, he thought that the injections on Elizabeth Barlow's left side had been given only hours before her death — much later than the ones on her right side. The first comparison test proved conclusively that Dr. Price had been right. The tissues from the woman's left side contained the larger quantity of unabsorbed insulin.

And even more data could be gleaned from this test. Reactions of the control mice allowed Curry to measure the unabsorbed residue of the dosages that had killed Elizabeth Barlow. Eighty-four units of insulin remained in the injection-site tissue. Since some of the insulin would have been absorbed into the bloodstream, the amount of insulin given to Elizabeth Barlow must have been many times greater — a dose purposefully and skillfully lethal.

But Curry wasn't satisfied at stopping with the results from these first tests. He was breaking new scientific ground, and he wanted to make sure his facts were right to the highest degree of probability before taking them into any court proceeding. So he ran four more complicated laboratory tests using various lab animals. Results from these tests piled evidence on the hypothesis that Elizabeth Barlow had been injected with a lethal dose of insulin.

Meanwhile biochemist S. S. Randall was investigating the case from another angle. He wondered if there were any substances besides insulin that could lead to a rapid breakdown of blood sugar. Were there any other substances that could produce the same symptoms of hypoglycemia as those displayed by Elizabeth Barlow?

He asked representatives of the pharmaceutical industry that question. He also asked specialists in diabetes. Both groups of scientists said there were such substances.

Randall undertook experiments with those substances. He found some that produced lowering of the blood-sugar level. But they did not produce the same symptoms as insulin.

There was no way that defense attorneys could argue that Elizabeth Barlow's death had been caused by anything but insulin.

The forensic scientists, and the experts upon whom they'd called for advice and information in the Elizabeth Barlow case, had patiently eliminated all possible reasons for her death one by one. Now only one further possible reason for Elizabeth Barlow's death remained to be investigated. A tumor of the pancreas, the gland that produces natural insulin, could suddenly, fatally, inject too much insulin into the blood. A person's body could literally kill itself if this happened.

But this cause of death was quickly ruled out. Examination of the woman's pancreas had already shown no signs of a tumor. Also, any such natural gush of insulin would have shown up evenly throughout the woman's body. It would not have collected at the injection sites.

So there it was! The conclusive proof that both Dr. Price and Curry were after.

The scientists were finally convinced that Kenneth Barlow had murdered his wife with an injection of insulin. And they had the proof they needed to convince a judge and jury of that fact, too. It had taken almost two months of dogged work, but their effort had brought them certainty.

Then a brand-new question reared itself up like a striking cobra. Until this question was answered to the scientists' satisfaction, Kenneth Barlow could still wriggle out of the justice he deserved.

This time the question arose from an unexpected place — work done by other Harrogate scientists in another case. The question dealt with the use of insulin as a perfect murder weapon.

A few years before, Barlow had said in conversation that insulin disappeared completely in the blood stream. When he said that, he had reflected current medical opinion. In the years since then, however, Harrogate forensic scientists had been able to get insulin extracts from a body many days after the person had died. In the light of that process, Curry asked himself, why hadn't he found any insulin in Elizabeth Barlow's body? Why had the presence of insulin been revealed only at the injection sites?

But the forensic scientists working on the Elizabeth Barlow case soon found the answer they needed to close the case to any further legal arguments. Not everything shuts down when a person dies. In the interior of the body, enzymes continue to work, breaking down proteins like insulin and thus producing alkaline tissues. In muscle, on the other hand, lactic acid develops after death. Insulin is stable in acidic body tissues.

After death, then, insulin is destroyed in the body's interior, but preserved in the outer muscles. And that is why Elizabeth Barlow's muscles had retained the injected insulin long enough for it to be found.

Finally, all the questions about a new and deadly use of a medicine had been answered to the scientists' satisfaction. The investigation ended.

The next day, Detective Superintendent Cheshire of Scotland Yard was able to take action. Cheshire had been part of the investigation, and it was his duty to charge Kenneth Barlow with the killing of his wife.

Barlow responded coolly, insisting that he had given Elizabeth no injections at all. A few days later, he changed his mind. Every time he changed his story, Curry followed up with research that produced admissible evidence to disprove it. By December, 1957, the evidence was so overwhelming that Kenneth Barlow could be formally charged with the murder of his wife "by injection of insulin."

Barlow continued to deny the charge.

But after the scientific evidence, so painstakingly compiled by the scientists of Harrogate and the specialists with whom they'd consulted, was given during Barlow's trial, the jury took only minutes to bring in a verdict of guilty.

The judge sentenced Barlow to life imprisonment, saying, "You have been found guilty of a cold, cruel, and awfully premeditated murder which but for a high degree of detective ability would never have been found out."

The tenacity and perseverance shown by forensic scientists, cooperating scientific specialists, and law enforcement officials in this case is almost exhausting to read about. But that kind of dogged cooperation is needed. No single person — or even a single scientific speciality — can keep track of everything in the exploding supermarket of poisons.

Sheer numbers pose what seem to be insurmountable difficulties in keeping up for forensic toxicologists and scientists in related fields. Happily, however, science has also developed some aids in identifying these new poisons. And science has also discovered some space-age shortcuts in identifying not only the presence of some *old* poisons like arsenic, but also the amount in which they are present. To many of us, these new poison identification methods and tools — X-ray crystallography, column chromatography, the spectroscope, and the nuclear reactor — sound mysterious and even overwhelming. To criminologists, they're simply part of science — knowledge that's been hard-won through persistent, painstaking experimentation.

6
Forensic Chemistry: Clues in the Dust

By the late nineteenth century, the notion that crimes couldn't and shouldn't be solved through human reason was changing. In fact, it was gone. Instead, most educated people now thought that *all* of life's problems could be solved by precise thinking and scientific knowledge.

A young medical student in Edinburgh, Scotland, wholeheartedly embraced this idea. The student's name was Arthur Conan Doyle. Later, as a young doctor with time on his hands, this belief influenced his choice of a hobby. Instead of wasting his time between appointments, Conan Doyle began to write stories featuring a hero who embodied the new respect for human intellect. His hero was the super-detective Sherlock Holmes. Conan Doyle's stories about Holmes soon became immensely popular.

Sherlock Holmes's investigative method was highly intelligent, rational, and particular. He also used techniques not employed by investigators at that time — examining such details as the differences between types of pipe and cigar ash, or footsteps, or hand shapes, even types of dirt. It was a method that didn't fit precisely into any of the currently accepted approaches to detective work. In fact, the way Sherlock Holmes worked broke new ground, paving the way for a whole new branch of criminology, one that was larger in scope than anything that had come before.

By 1893, Conan Doyle had run out of story ideas and had begun to find Holmes tiresome. He wrote a story to finish off his detective, flinging Holmes to his death in the gorge of the Reichenbach. But public outcry was so strong, Doyle was forced to resurrect him.

Eventually, the character Sherlock Holmes passed away. But his investigative method was reborn in print in 1907, when a serious, professional book called *Manual for Examining Magistrates* was published. The book was written by an Austrian named Hans Gross, who was himself a magistrate — his name for a criminologist.

Gross's book included chapters on the usual topics — toxicology, ballistics, and so on. But the book went much further, including chapters also on "Employment of the Chemist," "Employment of the Microscopist," and so on. Subtitles indicated in what areas Magistrate Gross thought the work of these specialists could be best used during crime investigations. One such subtitle was "Hair, Dust, Dirt on Shoes, Spots on Clothing."

The book was a huge success. A young French

scientist named Edmond Locard read both Gross's book and the Sherlock Holmes stories. He also listened to his teacher, Alexandre Lacassagne, Professor of Pathology and Forensic Medicine at the University of Lyons, lecture along the same lines.

Lacassagne proposed to his students that the dust on people's clothing, or in their ears and noses, or under their fingernails was valuable. Criminologists could use information gained by examining dust to their advantage in solving a crime. Dust could guide investigators to the whereabouts of suspects. It could give investigators information on suspects' occupations.

The idea that every criminal — thief, burglar, traffic offender, or murderer — came into contact with particles of dust at the scene of a crime excited the French scientist Locard. He decided to travel to as many of the world's crime labs as he could and go on tours through them. He wanted to discover what work was being done on dust and other trace clues.

Locard took his journey, but he didn't find as much information as he'd expected to find. Few crime labs were doing much with trace clues as yet. Still, the trip did add to Locard's excitement about the forensic possibilities of trace clues, and that excitement grew into a vision.

Once back home in Lyons in 1910, Locard tried to share his vision with police. They weren't interested. Leave the scientific, "glamorous" work to the big-city Sûreté investigators, the local police told Locard. The most they would give him were two dingy and rather sooty attic rooms in the Law Courts and two Sûreté officials as assistants.

But during the next two years, Locard proved the worth of his vision. He worked on cases that would soon bring him a lot of official support. The first of these cases dealt with counterfeiters.

For years, the Sûreté had been trying to find the source of a flood of false francs. Underworld informers had repeatedly given officials three names — Brun, Ceresk, and Latour. But it had been impossible for police to link these men with the counterfeit coins. Police couldn't even find their workshop! The only established fact in the case was the composition of the counterfeit coins. All the coins contained the same three ingredients — the metals tin and lead, and antimony, a chemical element with a silvery, metallic appearance that is commonly used in making metal alloys like those in coins.

Locard learned of the case and got in touch with Inspector Corin, the detective in charge. He asked for the clothing of the three suspects. Confused, Corin wanted to know why Locard would be asking for the men's clothes. Locard's request seemed silly to Inspector Corin, and he ignored it.

But Locard kept repeating his request. Finally, Corin decided it wasn't important enough to argue about. He relented and sent Locard the clothes of one suspect.

Eagerly but carefully, Locard examined all the pockets of the suspect's clothing under a magnifying glass, removing every metallic particle he found with a fine pincer. He brushed the suspect's sleeves over glossy white paper. The resulting dust showed up plainly on the paper, and Locard again painstakingly removed all the metallic particles.

Locard's next step was to ask two chemists working in Lyons for help. He asked them what the accepted way to determine the presence of antimony, tin, and lead was. The chemists gave Locard instructions, and Locard followed them exactly as he began testing the metallic particles he'd found in the dust on the suspect's clothing.

Very soon, lens-shaped crystals turned up in Locard's lab equipment. Many of these crystals were arranged in groups of three — the typical signs of antimony. Immediately, Locard began testing the dust from the suspect's clothes for tin and lead. In a short time, he verified the presence of both.

Now Inspector Corin was impressed. Locard had given him proof that the tips from informers were true! Now Corin was willing to cooperate with Locard in any way he could.

Without hesitation — but with an air of awe — Corin turned over to Locard the remaining suspects' clothing. The results of chemical tests on the dust of this clothing produced evidence that implicated these two suspects as well as the first.

The suspects were asked to account for the presence of the metallic particles on their clothes. When none of them could, they were all arrested. Confronted by the evidence, the suspects soon confessed to the counterfeiting.

Had the case been easier to solve, Locard might

not have impressed the police so much. But the case had been baffling, and the detectives who had worked on it were dumbfounded by Locard's seemingly supernatural abilities. Locard's success on that case astonished the police so much that it wasn't unusual for an investigator to come on his own to Locard's laboratory, arriving privately and without official orders, whenever he encountered a case that seemed to be unsolvable.

The solutions of further cases led to Locard's growing reputation as a "wizard" and brought ample official support in their wake. Locard was able to begin a large-scale scientific study of dust. His findings made a lasting contribution to criminology.

Twenty years after the day he first climbed the steep, winding staircase leading to his fourth-floor laboratory, Locard had acheived world fame. But he continued to work, still climbing the stairs every day. By then, his lab had grown larger, but it was still spottily heated by coal stoves spewing out soot, which settled in layers on the cracked walls.

By 1920, several younger scientists had taken up work in the field of dust research and were making reputations. One was a young chemist working in Berlin, Germany. His name was August Brüning.

Brüning had already achieved recognition by the time his work was interrupted by military service in World War I. So dedicated was he that he returned to his laboratory in the first postwar months.

Many of Brüning's new cases were thefts. After the war, Germany experienced shortages of many things, and people were eager to buy. That provided an incentive to steal things of worth. Some Berlin robbers became expert in stealing the valuable copper and bronze wire of telegraph and telephone lines.

Men wearing climbing shoes scaled the telegraph poles in the night. They cut down hundreds of yards of wire, rolled it up, and made a silent getaway on bicycles. They left the wire in hiding places known only to the "fences" who could sell it in the underground marketplace. Berlin police had trouble tracking down this group of robbers because they constantly changed the hiding places they used.

Then one day, the police happened to search a shack in a routine investigation. They came upon a knapsack that contained a large roll of copper wire. The shack was owned by a postal worker named Hermann Schalluk, who denied knowing anything about the contents of the knapsack. The knapsack itself, he said, belonged to a tramp he had taken pity on and put up for a night. Schalluk said that before he left, the tramp asked him to keep an eye on his knapsack.

Police didn't believe Schalluk's story. The postal worker's hands were suspiciously blackened, and police knew that the handling of many metals often leaves dark traces. Could the "clue hunter" Brüning help? It wouldn't hurt to take Schalluk to Brüning's offices, police thought, and they did.

In his lab, Brüning washed Schalluk's hands in hot, diluted hydrochloric acid. The man's hands instantly became clean. The blackening had been caused by dust particles that had accumulated in the ridges of the skin. Would examination of those dust particles prove that Schalluk had had more to do with that roll of copper wire than he claimed?

Brüning evaporated the hydrochloric acid from the solution that now contained those washed-off dust particles. The process left a yellow-green residue behind in the porcelain bowl. The residue contained almost pure copper chloride.

When confronted with this evidence, Schalluk explained that he had opened the knapsack out of curiosity and handled the roll of copper wire. He said adamantly that he certainly hadn't stolen the wire himself!

Schalluk's story could be true, but Brüning didn't think it was. He phoned the postal authorities for further information. When he learned that the wooden telegraph poles were soaked in copper sulfate, Brüning asked Schalluk to remove his trousers. If Schalluk was lying, if he had in fact climbed telegraph poles in the commission of a robbery, traces of copper sulfate would be found clinging to his trousers.

When Brüning examined Schalluk's trousers under the microscope, he discovered particles of wood along the part of the trouser leg that covered the inner thigh. He collected these particles, soaked them in a solution of ammonium nitrate, then heated them until they turned to ash. A chemical reaction quickly showed the presence of copper in the ashes. It had come from the copper sulfate the wooden poles had been treated with. Confronted with conclusive evidence, Schalluk confessed he had stolen the wire himself the night before.

Brüning had scored another triumph! Testing the clothing of suspected wire thieves immediately became the standard — and successful — police practice in Berlin.

So the scientists who searched for — and found — clues in the dust were proven to be on the right track. It was indisputably true that every criminal took something away from the scene of a crime.

The reverse is also true — a criminal always leaves something behind at the scene of a crime. What's left may be dust, fingerprints, body cells that can lead to DNA prints, or other microscopic clues such as glass, paint chips or traces, fibers, and so on.

For example, hit-and-run drivers usually leave minute traces of car paint on their victims. At the same time, their victims usually leave minute traces of fibers from their clothing on the car. Crime laboratories throughout the world are now able to solve crimes using these scraps of evidence.

Say that a flake of paint is left on a hit-and-run victim. Microscopic examination of this paint flake can determine the number of layers of pigment in the flake. Or a paint flake from the victim can be placed between the electrodes of a spectroscope and vaporized. That process can identify the composition of the paint — and from there, the make, model, and year of the hit-and-run car.

This astonishing determination is possible because of both science and computerized record-keeping. In 1975, the American Law Enforcement Assistance Administration began a plan to supply car paint samples to crime labs. Hundreds of samples of paint were sent out. The samples led to the arrests of so many hit-and-run drivers — and other kinds of criminals who had dragged their victims into cars — that the program was expanded. A simple computer run of car registrations matching the paint identification results in a list of suspects police can investigate.

In their investigation, police look for suspicious dents, dings, paint touch-up jobs, and anything else that can tie a particular car to a hit-and-run victim. This might be a fiber snagged on a side mirror. Use of a spectrophotometer in the lab can match fibers from the mirror with fibers from an article of the victim's clothing. Such conclusive evidence often draws a confession from a driver who had hoped to run from an accident altogether.

7
Forensic Entomology: Clues in Bugs

Some divers who were exploring the Muskegon River in Newaygo, Michigan, in the summer of 1989 discovered a whole lot more than they had bargained for — and what they found led to the conviction of a murderer.

While moving through the river water, the divers spotted a submerged car. Curious, they came closer, moving around the car to peer into it through the windshield.

Inside was the body of a dead woman. The divers immediately decided that they had found enough. They left their exploration and contacted police, who arrived to haul the car from the water.

Police set about tracing the car, soon discovering that it belonged to the husband of the dead woman. Medical examiners studied the body and found marks on the woman's head. The marks indicated that her death had been caused by violence.

When questioned, the husband said he didn't

know a lot about what had happend to his wife. He reported that the couple had had an argument a couple of weeks earlier, in June, and that his wife became upset. He said she had gotten into the car and driven away that night. It had been a foggy night, and the man told investigators that he imagined his wife had become disoriented in the mist and driven into the river. He added that he hadn't seen her since she left the house.

The police didn't believe the man's story. There were those marks on the woman's head, for one thing. They didn't seem to square with the kinds of injuries she would have sustained if her car had plunged into the river.

For another thing, neighbors had told police that they thought the woman had been gone for much longer than a couple of weeks. They said they hadn't seen her for months.

When police discovered that the husband had taken out a life insurance policy on his wife, they knew they had found a good motive for murder. The husband would collect a lot of money if his wife were dead.

And when police learned that the man had pawned his wife's jewelry, they became increasingly sure he was lying. They only needed to find one loose end in the husband's web of lies in order to unravel it. In this investigation, the loose end the police found to tug at was the time of death.

The river water was cold enough to have preserved the woman's body. That made determining her date of death difficult. But what police lost because of the water temperature was balanced by what they gained from it. Attached to the formerly submerged car's fenders were the pupal cocoons and larval cases of insects that lived in water.

Police knew that clues could be found in bugs, especially clues about the time of death. They sent the cocoons and larval case specimens to entomologist Richard Merritt of Michigan State University. Entomologists study insects, and Merritt's specialty was aquatic insects.

The cocoons were empty; the insects had already flown away. But Merritt easily identified signs of black flies, midges, and caddis flies. From the black fly cocoons, Merritt could work out approximately when the car had gone into the river.

The scientist based his statement on what he knew of the life cycle of the black fly. The larvae of these insects spend the winter in water. In spring, each of the larvae weaves a cocoon around itself, then attaches it to some stationary, solid base. Sometimes that's a rock in the bottom of the water. In this case, it was the fender of a sunken car. Inside its cocoon, the larva develops into an adult with wings. When this process of pupation is complete, the now-adult insect emerges to fly off, mate, and continue the cycle.

Merritt knew that the black fly species emerges from its cocoon, or pupates, in late April and May. "I knew the car must have gone into the river no later than that," he told police. "If it had gone into the river in June, as the husband claimed, it would not have had the cocoons on its fenders."

Now the police were sure that the husband had lied. They investigated further, in order to find the evidence they needed to present a case against him in court that would result in a conviction. They wanted to prove that the man had killed his wife, then faked a "fatal accident" by sending the car into the river.

On April 16, 1990, the man stood trial in the courthouse in White Cloud, Michigan. The evidence against him was based partly on the life cycle of the black fly. After hearing the evidence, the jury brought in a verdict of guilty.

Evidence from insects is a very recent development in criminology. In fact, the field known as forensic entomology was unknown in the United States ten years ago. By 1992, fewer than twenty scientists practiced this specialty, which is often used to establish the time of death of a body.

Before then, medical examiners had few ways to establish time of death with any degree of certainty. They could offer an expert opinion based on the presence or absence of rigor mortis, the temporary rigidity of muscles that occurs after death. They also could use chemical tests that were accurate for the first forty-eight hours after death. The trouble with those tests was that they were accurate for *only* the first forty-eight hours.

Today, when investigators are dealing with a body that has been dead for longer than that, they agree that bugs are a better help than anything else. The investigation, however, is not likely to appeal to anyone who doesn't have a strong stomach.

Swarming maggots are the stuff of nightmares and horror movies; they were often considered a disgusting nuisance by homicide squads in the past. But no longer!

The reason for the new importance of insect evidence in the investigation of a crime of violence that has left a dead body is that bugs follow a strict timetable in dealing with death. Entomologists can trace the predictable routine of these "natural undertakers" backwards in time and arrive at a more precise time of death than even a medical examiner with long experience. In one murder case in Chicago, for example, the coroner estimated that the victim had been dead for six weeks. The insect evidence said it was closer to six days — and the bugs turned out to be right.

The key to this investigative technique is keeping track of succession. Succession is the timing and life stages of insects as they feed and develop in a cadaver, or dead body. The case of the cocoons on the fenders of the faked car crash in Michigan described earlier was "clean." It hinged on knowledge of the life stages of insects outside the dead body.

Insects on and in a cadaver also have life stages that provide vital clues in solving crimes. The life cycles of these insects within the larger nutrient cycle of Earth are fixed and precise. They act as a natural clock. Expert reading of that clock can pinpoint the time of death precisely, even over many years.

Insect evidence arises as part and parcel of the nutrient cycle in which nature "hides" and recycles dead bodies. When an animal or a person dies in the open air, for example, microbes and bacteria immediately start feeding on the corpse. This causes the body to decay. The blowfly, a bright blue and green fly, has an extremely sensitive sense of smell. It detects the decaying tissue almost immediately.

From that point, the piling up of intricate and complicated heaps of insect evidence is inevitable *and* timeable. If it weren't, forensic entomology wouldn't be worth mentioning. Because of its growing importance, however, this field of criminal investigation is worthy of note, even though it may sound distasteful to some people.

The timetable works like this: Within ten minutes of death, swarms of blowflies and other flies including flesh flies, have appeared and already deposited thousands of eggs in the body's mouth, nose, and ears. Usually about twelve hours later, the eggs hatch into maggots that feed on the body's tissues. When the maggots finish, they will cocoon in the nearby soil. They move away from the cadaver, making room for the second wave of insects, usually beetles.

This wave of insects have come to feast on the now drying skin. Later, still more insects — spiders, mites, and millipedes — arrive. They have come for one of two reasons. They may prey on the bugs already at the site. Or they may also work at the remains of the body.

When police find insects crawling on a dead body, they collect samples and preserve them in alcohol. The kinds of insects and their stages of development lead to the knowledge of how long the body has been dead.

There are othere facts police must consider, of course. If someone dies at night, for example, blowflies won't deposit their eggs on the body until dawn. If the weather has been too hot or too cold, the blowflies will themselves be dead and incapable of leaving any evidence on the body. But even this lack of evidence can speak loudly, as it did in one 1987 case.

This case shows the value of insect evidence over long periods of time. The case is, in fact, the longest interval between death and discovery of victims in which bugs played a major role, although the role was played in absentia.

It seems officials had learned that an elderly man had died of natural causes in his Midwestern home. When they went to his house to investigate, they were surprised to find not just one corpse, but three! The man's aunt and niece were found lying in their beds. The two women's bodies were completely dried out, and apparently they had been lying there like mummies for years. There was no sign of insect activity on them. An entomologist suspected that the two women had died years before during a long cold spell.

The entomologist was right. Police found a diary belonging to one of the women. The last entry was dated October 4, 1977. A little more research disclosed that the winter of 1977–78 had, in fact, been unusually cold. The frigid weather had allowed the bodies to dry out rather than decay. That accounted for the insect evidence, which was, in this case, eloquent by its absence.

The crime here was not murder. The man had simply never reported the deaths of his relatives. Instead, he'd been collecting the dead women's social security checks and keeping the money — some 140,000 dollars — for himself.

Knowing the time of death can solve many different kinds of cases than murder. And insects can uncover far more than just the time of death.

For example, bugs can point to a killer. Entomologist Neal Haskell, of Purdue University, describes one case in which police found the body of a dead woman in a shallow grave. A forensic entomologist calculated that she had died before sundown the previous Wednesday, based on the growth stage of blowfly maggots on the body. Three men were suspects, but only one of them had been in town at the time of her death. He was accused of the crime.

William Rodriguez, a forensic anthropologist with the Armed Forces Institute of Pathology in Washington, DC, was instrumental in "reading the bugs" in another case. Two convicts were discussing a murder committed ten years earlier. The conversation was overheard, and a public investigation followed. The body was recovered. With that, the two convicts started accusing each other of the homicide. Each man told investigators the other's confession. The major difference between the two confessions was the season during which the murder was committed.

Rodriguez went to the gravesite. He found no evidence of insect activity on the body. That led him to determine that the killing had occurred in winter. This and other evidence led to a conviction of the real killer.

Bug behavior can even help scientists recreate the scene of a crime. Some species of insects will lay eggs only indoors. Or at high noon. Or in warm weather. Others may prefer cool locations, or shade, or moisture. Collection of crime clues based on the behaviors of an insect species can determine if a victim was killed indoors or outdoors, if the murder took place during the day or at night, if the weather was warm or cool during the murder, or whether the murder took place in the shade or in the sun.

Another characteristic of bug behavior is that bugs tend to stick around their homes. Their presence on a body can often tell investigators if the scene of a murder was the same as the site at which the body was found. If a city bug shows up on a cornfield corpse, for example, it's a safe bet the body has been transported from city to country. In fact, entomologists can often specify not only from which city the corpse was brought, but also the neighborhood in which the murder must have taken place.

For many years, the decaying or fly-infested bodies of victims of ugly crimes were cleaned up before medical examiners began to work. That no longer routinely happens. These days, the insect evidence is simply too valuable to ignore. Such evidence is rapidly becoming respected in the courtroom, and it promises to become even more important in the future.

Entomologists say they now understand the behaviors of only about half the insect species that frequent corpses. They're working to increase that data base, and it is growing. Forensic entomologists are also beginning to use computer simulations. These make quicker and more sophisticated investigations possible. One forensic entomologist predicts that one day even the bug stains on automobile windshields will yield investigative gold!

8

A New Criminology: Psychological Profiling

Until the 1970s, police investigating a murder case could be fairly certain that the victim and the killer were linked in some way. In around eighty percent of killings, the crime had emerged from a relationship, and police solved homicide cases by tracing a link between victim and killer.

Another thing police could be fairly certain of was that the killer had had something to gain from the death of the murdered person. Until the late nineteenth century, most murders were committed for profit. After asking where the victim's spouse was at the time the killing was committed, the next question that popped into a police officer's mind was usually, "Who stood to gain economically by getting the dead person out of the way?" Answers to that question most often led police to a good suspect, the best starting place for finding the facts needed to take a case to court and win a conviction.

These certainties were really only rule-of-thumb

generalities. They worked in most cases. In point of fact, the certainty of a link between killer and victim had ended in 1888 when Jack the Ripper began murdering in the Whitechapel section of London.

The Ripper was one of the first of a violent breed of criminals that came to be known as serial killers. Never caught, the Ripper simply stopped killing for reasons no one would ever know. Even his identity is still unknown. That is one of the greatest unsolved mysteries of all times.

After the Ripper's murder career ended, other serial killers came along from time to time. Still, such killers were few and far between. In the 1970s all that changed — in the United States and in the world.

In the United States, the 1970s were unsettling times. The controversy surrounding our involvement in the undeclared war in Vietnam continued to rage. And for the first time, in 1974 a United States president was impeached.

Newspaper headlines and the lead stories on the nightly television news focused on events rising from this political turmoil. Another alarming situation went unnoticed: The proportion of random killings was on the rise.

In the mid-1960s, random killings were only six percent of the total homicides. By the mid-1970s, the percentage of random killings had tripled, rising to eighteen percent of total homicides. By the mid-1980s, one expert estimate said that 5,000 persons were being killed each year by total strangers.

And there was another disturbing statistic. The solution rate for homicides was dropping. About ninety percent of homicides were solved in the late 1940s, when law enforcement officials could still count on there being a link between murderer and victim. Only ten percent of the homicide cases went unsolved, their case files never able to be stamped "Closed." By 1983, that picture had changed drastically. Twenty-eight percent of homicides were never solved.

The diminishing ability of law enforcement officials to solve homicides wasn't due to a quantum leap in police stupidity. Instead, it suggested that a whole new game was afoot, a game in which commonly accepted criminological approaches no longer worked well. As the link between murderer and victim unraveled, chance or luck came to be the most usual means of solving many puzzling homicides.

Police continued to work doggedly, continuing to think that the Boston Strangler, Charles Manson and his infamous family, "Zodiac," and other serial killers were weirdos, individual aberrations in the rest of a predictable, understandable fabric of society.

But then something clicked. Suddenly, police recognized that they were dealing with a new kind of killer. Many crime historians point to 1973 as the year the "click" happened, and they see the Dean Corll case as the cause.

As police investigated the murder of Dean Corll, in Houston, Texas, they made a horrifying discovery. The murdered man had killed at least twenty-seven victims. By the time the investigation was complete, they realized the number was more than thirty. Shocked, police realized that, for Dean Corll, murder had become a habit. The habit had been stopped by the person who refused to continue "supplying" Corll with victims.

The new breed of killer was appearing in other nations, too. But the FBI was concerned solely with what was happening in America. And in 1984, FBI officials admitted that there was an "epidemic" of serial murders in our country. Since serial killers were a new everyday phenomenon, combating them called for new investigative tools and methods.

Psychologist Joel Norris had done extensive research on cases of serial murder. It put him in a good position to help define what was going on in the minds of serial killers.

Norris was able to identify some things all serial killers had in common. He found most were "physically and psychologically damaged people." They themselves had been no strangers to violence directed at them. As children, most had been abused by alcoholic parents or adults addicted to other drugs.

So serial killers were also familiar with addictive behaviors. They knew no other way to get through the stresses of life. They themselves had become addicts — but with a terrible twist. Serial killers had become addicted to murder. "On his own initiative, the serial killer can no more stop killing than a heroin addict can kick the habit," Norris concluded.

Yet Norris also concluded that all serial killers wished for some way to stop doing what they were doing. They wished for death. In fact, the prospect of electrocution or lethal injection didn't deter them from continuing to kill. Instead, the notion of capital punishment, of being legally put to death and giving their life for the lives they had taken, served as an inducement to them to continue killing. Murdering was a way to get caught. Deep down that's what they wanted.

But they also wanted something else. Norris felt that serial killers believed in their own superhuman importance. The world had treated them badly, but they could get back what they'd needed and hadn't been given by proving their superiority in a series of murders. Killing evened out the balance; it made them feel good.

Like other addicts, serial killers soon found that they needed more and more of what made them feel good in order to maintain that feeling. To protect their "supply" — in this case freedom of access to victims — serial killers put on what Norris called a "mask of sanity." In other words, the new breed of killers behaved in a way that would make society see them as model citizens.

That means they didn't draw attention to themselves as being possible criminals. Instead, they did just the opposite. For example, serial killer John Gacy was a successful building contractor and often performed as a clown in the children's wards of hospitals. Serial killer Wayne Williams ran an advertising agency and was featured in Atlanta newspapers and on television programs. Serial killer Ted Bundy was a law student, an employee of several prestigious crime investigation organizations, and a successful, highly regarded political volunteer.

Dr. Norris's work resulted in psychological profiles of serial killers. He felt these were valuable because they could lead to a predictive test. Individuals who might be at risk of becoming addicted to killing could be identified early and helped before they began a life of crime.

The FBI was interested in psychological profiles from a different point of view. They wondered if these profiles coul 1 be used to catch criminals. With that in mind, the special agents of the Behavioral Science Unit (BSU), which is part of the FBI's National Center for the Analysis of Violent Crime, began looking at crime-scene clues in a different light. No longer was evidence only a record of what had been done. Now the evidence became a symptom of the sickness of the person who had committed the crime.

One special agent, Roy Hazelwood, expressed the view that rather than getting hung up on *why* a killer does something, focusing on *how* it's done would best track down the killer. This did not mean that physical evidence was overlooked. If anything, it was scrutinized even more carefully than before. The tiniest clue in the mound of evidence in a case could focus its investigation by shedding light on the psychology of the killer. The evidence in a single case could be analyzed through a filter of what was known about the personality and behavioral characteristics of killers in *all* cases. This process was called "criminal profiling."

BSU special agents began looking at eight-by-ten color photos of the scene as if they were photos of the criminal's mind. They studied reports from police on the scene, and summaries of those reports, for their superiors from the "criminal profile" slant. They took the same point of view as they read the other case paperwork like autopsy protocols, reports from labs, and statements of all those who'd been questioned.

The BSU special agents were not detectives themselves. They were scientists seeking to describe the kind of individual who might have committed a particular kind of crime. They diagnosed the serial killer's mental illness — his compulsion to kill — from the psychological "prints" he left at a crime scene. In doing so, they worked much as a medical doctor diagnosing a physical illness through its symptoms.

In making a diagnosis, a medical doctor has a wealth of data to draw on. For example, if a patient comes to a medical doctor complaining of numb hands and toothache or pain in the jaw, the doctor will note that these symptoms often point to heart problems. The doctor will investigate that serious possibility first.

In order to work in the same way, the FBI had to compile its own data bank of symptoms shown by various kinds of criminals. To do that with one kind of serial killer, they interviewed thirty-six convicted serial killers of that type. All of the serial killers studied by the FBI were men. In fact, the majority of *all* serial killers are men.

Why did the thirty-six killers agree to talk with the FBI interviewers?

None of them had anything to lose by telling the truth since they had exhausted all avenues of legal appeal. There was no legal way they could get their convictions overturned now.

But, on the other hand, all thirty-six killers had something to gain by talking about their crimes. Their murders had been compulsive, the acts of a murder addict. They had been driven to committing them by fantasies. Answering the interviewers' well-defined questions was another way for these men to relive their crimes, to get a repeat of the "buzz" they'd gotten while committing them.

What emerged from these interviews was summed up in the August 1985 issue of *FBI Law Enforcement Bulletin*. A new link between victim and killer became clear — murder sprang from fantasies about mastering other people. "Acting out the fantasy links the fantasy to reality, and the fantasy *becomes* reality. The offender believes he can now control reality," the FBI interviewers concluded.

That was the new link between killer and victim. No longer was it a real relationship, like husband and wife or brother and sister, as it had been in the past. For serial killers, the link between their violence and their victims was finding some unsuspecting person to become an actor in the killer's own private daydream!

The interviews conducted by the behavioral scientists of the FBI's BSU sketched in the killers' backgrounds. Scientists began to see what kinds of people became serial killers. The interviews also showed how the symptoms of an individual killer's mental illness would show up at the scene of the crime he'd committed.

One set of these symptoms defined a killer as either organized or disorganized. As the category names indicate, the organized killer planned his crimes, whereas the disorganized killer just happened into them. These differences in approach are clearly identifiable.

Is the body hidden? Organized killer at work.

Has the weapon been taken away? Organized killer at work.

The organized killer has planned his attack. The disorganized killer, on the other hand, strikes spontaneously. He kills his victim in a location he knows. He attempts to depersonalize the victim after death in some way, sometimes by bludgeoning the face. Then he bolts from the scene of his crime, leaving his weapon and the body in plain view. The crime scene is random and sloppy.

Evidence at the crime scene tips off investigating officers about the killer's degree of organization. And that tells police a lot about the personality characteristics they can look for in their suspects.

In part, the FBI describes an organized killer as

being of average intelligence or above. He knows how to get along with people in daily life and he prefers skilled work. He was born first or second in his family. His father's work was unstable, and he received inconsistent discipline as a child. Sometimes he was punished for doing something, for example, while other times doing the same thing went unnoticed.

The organized killer's mood was controlled during the crime, although his decision to commit a crime may have been fueled by the use of alcohol. His crime was triggered by stress. He is living with a partner. He is mobile, and his car is in good condition. He takes an interest in the crime he has committed, following it through reports in the newspapers and on television broadcasts. He may change jobs and leave town after his crime(s).

The disorganized killer, on the other hand, has below average intelligence, and he's likely to work at unskilled jobs. He doesn't get along well with other people in daily life because he often doesn't know what to say or how to say it. He has at least two older brothers or sisters, and he received harsh discipline as a child. He doesn't use alcohol during his crimes. He feels anxious as he kills. He lives alone and has little interest in the news reporting of his crime(s). His home or workplace is near the crime scene. His behavior changes significantly after he's committed his crime(s).

Will all this help police catch a serial killer?

Probably not by itself.

But expert questioning of suspects can pinpoint

the mental illness and thus narrow down the field of suspects. Serial killers, for example, will often use the word "he" instead of the word "I" when asked to speculate on the nature of a person capable of doing what they are being questioned about having done. They use an imaginary third person in order to deny their guilt. In other words, they *are* the "he" they're speculating about.

After his conviction, serial killer Ted Bundy, for example, used the word "he" instead of the word "I" when he speculated at great length about his own crimes. He talked this way to two journalists, Stephen G. Michaud and Hugh Aynesworth, who were writing a book about him.

Note this example of Bundy's "speculations" from Michaud and Aynesworth's book, *The Only Living Witness*, published in 1983: "In his readings and his observations and what-have-you — in his fantasy world — he'd imagined for some reason people disappearing all the time. He was aware of how people dropped out and became runaways and whatnot. In devising his scheme, he'd taken this somewhat unrealistic conclusion that under the correct circumstances he could select any person as a victim and that there'd be virtually no attention paid. . . . He was always amazed and chagrined by the publicity generated by disappearances he thought would go almost totally unnoticed."

Bundy would not admit guilt. "I feel sorry for people who feel guilt," he said.

Other serial killers in the FBI's interviews also used an imaginary third person or being in order to deny their guilt. One of these was the Son of Sam, who had gotten that name because that's how he signed the warning notes he had written and sent out. His signature came about because, he said, he was simply following orders to stalk his victims that had been issued by his neighbor's dog, Sam. Interestingly enough, when the BSU interviewer told the killer to stop being silly, the Son of Sam began to talk about himself in his true identity as David Berkowitz.

One reason criminal profiles weren't especially useful in the past in helping police arrest serial killers like Bundy, is that serial killers were mobile. Bundy, for example, had driven far and wide in a Volkswagen "bug" looking for slim, pretty young women with long dark hair parted in the middle. Notorious in the northwestern states, Bundy was unknown in Florida — so unknown that when he was picked up by chance in Pensacola, the police who questioned him didn't even recognize his name. Clearly, the lack of a centralized, national police communications system had helped Bundy's killing career enormously.

In July 1983, Senate hearings in Washington, DC, were undertaken to fund and put into place a new communications system. The hearings were about the need for the adoption of a Violent Criminal Apprehension Program (VICAP) as part of the FBI's Behavioral Science Unit. The VICAP program would computerize data about violent crimes that had taken place all over the nation. It would make this information available to local police working on apparently unsolvable cases. And it could stop serial killers before mere chance led them into the hands of the police.

Ann Rule, a witness at these hearings, spoke from her experience as a former police officer, a full-time author of true-crime books, and her own familiarity with the Ted Bundy case.

She said, "The thing that I have found about the serial murderers that I have researched is that they travel constantly, they are trollers. While most of us might put 15,000 to 20,000 miles a year on our cars, several of the serial killers I have researched have put 200,000 miles a year on their cars. They move constantly. They might drive all night long. They are always looking for the random victim who may cross their path."

Rule went on to say that the lives of fourteen to fifteen victims could have been saved if a central pool of information had been available to Utah police, who had arrested Bundy early in his murder career.

As a result of these hearings, VICAP was funded. By the end of 1989, the data bank contained information on approximately 3,700 cases from the United States, Canada, and other countries. It is now possible for a local or state law enforcement agency to compare a homicide case it is investigating with hundreds of others, in a number of different categories.

VICAP data banks are arranged by different criteria. One is categories of murder. Another deals with the primary intent of the murderer. The Offender Risk File contains information on the kind and extent of the risks taken by the killer in the process of his crime. The Victim Risk File shows what about the victim brought them to the attention of the killer. The Escalation File is an analysis of facts and patterns of solved crimes, showing the sequence of events. Time and Location Factors are analyzed and filed. Crime Scene Dynamics have been compiled — the killer's style, his symptoms, his personality.

In 1989 alone, VICAP took an active part in 793 cases. Their help offered law enforcement officers included not only criminal profiles, but also guidance in areas ranging from the questioning of suspects to courtroom strategies.

But as former FBI Director William S. Sessions points out, "Computer technology cannot replace the human element in conducting investigations and analyzing crime." What has been called the "blue sense" — the intuitive hunches that good, seasoned cops acquire — can't be replaced by computers, but emerging forensic techniques can certainly guide "blue sense" into the best use of time and effort.

9
The Future

Emerging forensic techniques cover a lot of ground. Many crime historians think that psychology is the most interesting and productive development in crime detection in the second half of the twentieth century. They feel that the insights gained from criminal profiling can offer a key to healing the criminal mind.

Can crimes be stopped by curing the mind?

Dan MacDougald thinks so. MacDougald is a penologist, a criminologist who deals with prison management and the treatment of offenders.

MacDougald heard one day of an experiment performed at Harvard University by Dr. Bernard Jouvet. Jouvet had connected the aural nerve from a cat's ear to an oscilloscope. When a sharp click sounded in the cat's ear, the oscilloscope registered the vibration of the cat's eardrum. The vibration told Jouvet that the cat had heard the click.

Then Jouvet placed a jar with white mice in front

of the cat. Now something very different happened. The cat not only ignored the click, but the oscilloscope's needle didn't move!

It stood to reason that even if the cat ignored the click, the sound waves should have traveled to its eardrum and from there to the oscilloscope. Instead, what was happening was that the cat was cutting out the sound at its eardrum. The cat was somehow able to *not* hear.

MacDougald wondered if this is what criminals did. There was evidence in an earlier psychiatric theory developed by Dr. Samuel Yochelson to support this idea.

Yochelson had begun a study of criminals in St. Elizabeth's Hospital in Washington, DC, working with a young colleague named Stanton E. Samenow. The two had begun their work thinking that criminals were the way they were because of deep-seated psychological problems. But as they continued to work, the two found themselves changing their minds.

They began thinking that the central traits of the criminal personality were weakness, immaturity, and self-delusion. These undesirable traits were mixed with a strong desire to deceive other people. They also found that criminals had no desire to change. The minute they left the doctor's office, they went straight back to being criminals again. They also had great skill in self-justification and could easily "psych out" and manipulate doctors.

Criminals also had a "shut-off mechanism" that let them ignore or forget anything they wanted to ignore or forget. They could admit to something in one session, then swear up and down at the next that they'd never said that.

In addition, criminals lacked self-discipline. They were cowards. They would, for example, allow their teeth to rot before they'd face a dentist's drill. There were other things that frightened them, too. They feared someone else would see their weaknesses. They overreacted when someone said something to "put them down."

The only way to get criminals to change was to help them see that their behavior didn't help them achieve what they wanted to achieve. Something like a religious conversion was needed. The best time to achieve that was when something a criminal *didn't* want was staring him in the face. That could be something like the beginning of a long jail term, or it could be when the criminal was feeling self-disgust.

Those were some of the points at which criminals could be reminded that they had three options — crime, suicide, or change — and they could choose which. If they chose change, the way was clear. The steps they needed to take were these:

- Turn off their "shut-off mechanism."
- Accept that their present system of dealing with life wasn't working well.
- Switch to a new system.

That made sense to MacDougald. He was seeing a pattern. The cat could shut off the click when it didn't want to hear it, and criminals shut off the results of their crimes when they don't want to hear them.

For example, when a con man deceives someone to gain their money, he pushes his human feelings into another compartment. At first he may be a nice guy to his family and a con man to his victims. But given enough con-man experiences, he becomes less human with everybody. By acting on the notion that a sucker is born every minute, the con man soon creates that to be his complete reality. He is surrounded by suckers just waiting to be taken in. Even his own family became suckers.

MacDougald thought we all needed to change our thinking that the criminal is being dominated by an unjust society. Instead, thought MacDougald, a criminal is dominated by negative attitudes *toward* society.

You can't trust anybody, the criminal thinks, and this is how he literally *sees* thing. Nothing positive can enter his vision. Anything that contradicts his negative view of life is shut off.

Most people probably have one or two blind spots of negativity, but a criminal's whole vision is clouded with his. If a person could find a way to "open up" and enlighten that all-encompassing darkness of vision, MacDougald thought, then he could help criminals become aware of their faulty shut-off mechanism. Once that happened, criminals would stop being criminals. Criminal behavior just wouldn't make sense to them any longer.

But how to accomplish that?

MacDougald decided that the way to open up that faulty shut-off mechanism was to study how criminals used words like *law, honesty, neighbor, love,* and *self,* among others. The next step was to ask the criminal to explain himself until he began to see where he was going wrong.

Sound simple?

Too simple?

Perhaps.

But it appears to work.

Here's proof.

In 1967, MacDougald took his program into a maximum security prison near Reidesville, Georgia. He began working with hard-core psychopaths, men who had no use for anyone else other than to mess with them. In two weeks, impressive constructive changes had occurred in the twenty-two-man group. In eight weeks, sixty-three percent of the men in the group had been successfully rehabilitated. They didn't *want* to behave as they had in the past.

What happened next was even more impressive. This sixty-three percent of rehabilitated men became instructors of others. This group showed the same rate of success of rehabilitation.

What had happened was that in "unblocking" themselves, the men's self-esteem had risen.

MacDougald's assumption that criminality occurs when a person *under*values himself was proven correct. It was being proven true that a person can't love anyone else until he can love himself. And that a person who loves himself will stop criminal activities.

When MacDougald learned to diagnose the extent of a man's criminality from his "word blindness," he had developed a powerful technique.

Other law enforcement officials think that the best way to deal with criminals is through better forensic science. Crime is a reality, they say; it is always with us and always will be. Some of these people look to advances in new sciences, such as forensic entomology or forensic anthropology, to provide better ways to fight crime. Others look to technology.

One such technological advance applies to lie detectors, or polygraphs. The instrument is now almost infallible, although polygraph evidence has been inadmissible in most American courts since 1923. It can be used in court only if both sides agree, or if the judge demands it.

To Chris Gugas, founder of the National Board of Polygraph Examiners, the lack of admissibility of polygraph evidence is largely due to misuses of such evidence in the past.

He points to the results of a study of 4,280 criminals in the 1950s. A polygraph used by a trained expert was shown to be ninety-five percent accurate.

A polygraph shows when someone is telling a lie. But it can also show innocence. It can even detect a murderer if no questions at all are asked!

Gugas proved this in a case that took place in a Greek seaport.

Gugas had been sent there after World War II to train local police in new methods of crime detection. The chief of police felt the lie detector was a waste of time, but Gugas managed to win him and the other men over.

That was when Gugas heard of a case that interested him. A woman had disappeared. Her husband was a powerful local politician, and he was making life miserable for the police. He declared that he wanted his wife found, but was that really true?

The politician was so powerful, the Greek police didn't even want to question him. When Gugas heard the politician hadn't been questioned by authorities, he volunteered to do it himself.

He and some assistants went to the politician's house to ask some easily answered questions: "When were you first aware your wife was missing?" "Had your wife made any enemies recently?" "Was she planning a trip?"

The politician apparently found even these kinds of questions to be too inquisitive. He soon declared, "The interview is over!"

Now Gugas was sufficiently intrigued to want to follow the case to the bitter end. He learned that the politician had a lady friend and Gugas went to her house to ask her questions.

The politician didn't like this, either. In fact, he arranged for Gugas to meet with an American diplomat, who told Gugas to stop.

But Gugas didn't.

He kept nosing around until he learned that the politician's vanished wife owned a faraway estate. The remote estate was now deserted. Gugas immediately sent police photographers there with instructions to take as many pictures as possible.

Then Gugas called the politician's lawyer, saying that he would promise to leave the case if he could have just one more interview with the supposedly bereaved husband.

The lawyer said no, but the politician thought Gugas's deal sounded good. He showed up on his own. He even said Gugas could hook him up to the polygraph — on one condition. Gugas couldn't ask any questions.

Astonishingly, Gugas agreed.

During the meeting, Gugas stuck to his promise. Instead of asking the politician questions, Gugas showed the man the photographs of his wife's estate he'd had the police photographers take.

One by one Gugas raised and lowered the pictures. When Gugas raised the photo of the stables, the polygraph's indicator jumped. That's it! Gugas thought. He thanked the politician and sent him home.

In a very short time, Gugas had police digging at the stables. They soon disinterred the half-decomposed body of the politician's missing wife. The next step was clear — the politician was charged with his wife's murder. He was later convicted.

With its ninety-five percent accuracy rate when

used by a trained expert, the polygraph machine is as valuable to police as other technology, such as voice-printing devices.

Another long-time aid in the detection of crime is hypnosis. Like the results from a lie detector test, the information gained through hypnosis is often not admissible in court. But the use of hypnosis in many cases, including the Boston Strangler case, has given police valuable information.

How hypnotism works is still not completely understood, but its value in getting at the facts has been proven over and over again. Persons in highly traumatic situations like murder, car crashes, or burglaries may "block out" painful details in later ordinary life. But hypnosis somehow "unblocks" them. Under hypnosis, these people can supply precise details.

Hypnosis is so valuable, in fact, that many — if not most — crime investigators use it regularly. It can provide shortcuts that save police time and people lives. In this, hypnosis is like so many of the other technological forensic advances.

Even the best forensic science available, however, can't insure that there will be no miscarriages of justice in the future. A process as seemingly definite as identification through DNA prints remains prey to errors — mistakes in the laboratory, evidence "planted" at a crime scene, and so on. There will always be a shadow of doubt. Questions will continue to arise in court proceedings.

And that's where justice must go back to following someone's bloodhound instincts.

Before forensic science found acceptance and developed, crime investigators had to rely on these instincts. They had to sense where to look for criminals. They had to ground their guesswork in exhaustive, time-consuming, door-to-door, check-the-records legwork. This approach has been called the "needle-in-the-haystack" method.

There's nothing inherently wrong with this approach. After all, today's investigators also have to add their own crime-detection savvy to the mountains of data heaped up by technology.

And perhaps the best defense society has against the criminals who prey upon it will remain right where it has always been — in the intuitive "blue sense" of police and the magical courage of others who "smell a rat" and refuse to rest until it is ferreted out.